DANGEROUS LIAISONS

DANGEROUS LIAISONS:
FASHION AND FURNITURE IN THE EIGHTEENTH CENTURY

Harold Koda and Andrew Bolton
With an Introduction by Mimi Hellman

The Metropolitan Museum of Art, New York
Yale University Press, New Haven and London

This catalogue has been adapted from the exhibition "Dangerous Liaisons: Fashion and

Furniture in the 18th Century" held at The Metropolitan Museum of Art, New York,

from April 29 to September 6, 2004.

The exhibition and this catalogue are made possible by

Additional support has been provided by

CONDÉ NAST
PUBLICATIONS

Published by The Metropolitan Museum of Art, New York

Copyright © 2006 by The Metropolitan Museum of Art, New York

John P. O'Neill, Editor in Chief

Gwen Roginsky, Associate General Manager of Publications

Joan Holt, Editor

Paula Torres, Production Manager

Matsumoto Incorporated NY, Designers

Photography by Joseph Coscia Jr. and Oi-Cheong Lee of the Photograph Studio,

The Metropolitan Museum of Art

Color separations by Professional Graphics Inc., Rockford, Illinois

Printed and bound by Mondadori Printing S.p.A., Verona, Italy

Front cover: Detail of *The Masked Beauty* (see pp. 77–81)

Back cover: Detail of *The Shop* (see p. 122)

Frontispiece: *The Connoisseur*, photographed at the entrance of

The Wrightsman Galleries (see p. 117)

Cataloging-in-Publication Data is available from the Library of Congress.

ISBN: 1-58839-147-7 (The Metropolitan Museum of Art)

ISBN: 0-300-10714-5 (Yale University Press)

CONTENTS

Inspired by Jean-François de Bastide's erotic novella *La Petite Maison*, The Costume Institute's *Dangerous Liaisons* catalogue explores the idea that in eighteenth-century France fashion and furniture were intended to attract, arouse, and, ultimately, to seduce. It is fitting that Asprey, with a rich artistic heritage, supports a catalogue lauding a period that, in terms of the applied arts, has come to be seen as the apex of taste and refinement.

Founded in 1781, Asprey epitomizes aesthetic sophistication and exacting craftsmanship through its long tradition in china, silver, jewelry, glassware, and leatherwork. The premier maker of luxury goods in England, Asprey's royal patronage has included Queen Victoria and King Edward VII. Today, Asprey's reputation for artistic vision is upheld and advanced through the modern and innovative approach of its designers.

Asprey is proud to support this remarkable catalogue generated by The Metropolitan Museum of Art's Costume Institute.

In 1963 figures dressed in the attire of Louis XV and Louis XVI were placed in informal vignettes throughout the Museum's French period rooms, The Wrightsman Galleries. Since then, the rooms have benefited from a series of new acquisitions and gifts, many with exceptionally distinguished provenances, and all displaying the most refined artistry of the period. After more than four decades, "Dangerous Liaisons: Fashion and Furniture in the 18th Century" restated the strategy of that earlier installation, now greatly enhanced by the many additions to the rooms.

For the Metropolitan, the collaboration of our departments of European Sculpture and Decorative Arts and The Costume Institute is an important reflection of the collegiality and diversity of our curatorial expertise and the breadth of our holdings. This Museum is especially well-positioned for such interdepartmental "synergies." However, the narratives that linked the rooms in "Dangerous Liaisons" were a kind of theater, and unusual for an art museum. More typically, artworks are displayed with the understanding that their aesthetic merit and the virtuosity of their creators are better conveyed when they are separated spatially to underscore their uniqueness. Unlike natural-history dioramas or historical-society tableaux, presentation of works in an art museum is generally without recreation of their original social and cultural contexts.

Perhaps no one was more surprised than the contributing curators to see how the exceptional nature of their objects was enriched by such juxtapositions. To view the elaborately attired figures in the rooms was to understand the just proportions of the spaces. Such settings also served to link and unify the rarefied opulence of the furniture and costumes. Moreover, through these vignettes eighteenth-century conceits and social behavior were made more accessible and human because of the intimacy implicit in the playful narratives.

"Dangerous Liaisons" would not have been possible without its unparalleled settings and the masterworks assembled there by Jayne Wrightsman, whose generosity, knowledge, and insight have informed the evolution of the Museum's collection of eighteenth-century furniture and decorative arts. Most of the fine examples of eighteenth-century dress came from the superlative holdings of The Costume Institute, which were enhanced by rare works from the collections of Lillian Williams and the Kyoto Costume Institute.

"Dangerous Liaisons" was organized by Harold Koda, curator in charge of The Costume Institute, and Andrew Bolton, associate curator, who, along with Mimi Hellman, assistant professor of art history at Skidmore College, are the authors of this book adapted from the exhibition. Beautifully conceptualized and staged by Patrick Kinmonth and expertly photographed by Joseph Coscia Jr. and Oi-Cheong Lee, the vignettes that follow will certainly transport the reader back to this "age of allurement."

We are extremely grateful to Asprey for their generous support of both the exhibition and this book. We would also like to thank Condé Nast for their additional support of both projects.

Philippe de Montebello
Director, The Metropolitan Museum of Art

The exhibition "Dangerous Liaisons: Fashion and Furniture in the 18th Century," from which this book is derived, is the second instance of costume presented in The Wrightsman Galleries. While the first, "Costumes: Period Rooms Re-occupied in Style" (1963), also featured notable examples of eighteenth-century dress, they were presented in tableaux of neutral, sparely articulated narratives. Emphasis was placed on the clothing rather than the furniture and architectural components. For "Dangerous Liaisons," however, the curators elected a different approach, one intended to establish a more dynamic occupation of the rooms. Through a series of dramatic vignettes, equal prominence has been given to the apparel and the applied arts.

Philippe de Montebello has noted that the Metropolitan's period rooms, including The Wrightsman Galleries, "were installed principally . . . to display suites of furniture selected from the Museum's holdings and combined in the setting to express a particular style, rather than to reinvent the original room." With similar intentions, the curators of "Dangerous Liaisons," along with the exhibition's creative director, Patrick Kinmonth, staged tableaux that effected a stylistic relationship between fashion and furniture in the eighteenth century. The scenes allude to the carefully cultivated appearances and accomplished behaviors in codified rituals that characterized the social activities of the French nobility of the period. To further emphasize the artifice and theatrical nature of the scenarios, Kinmonth introduced footlights to the existing diffuse daylight and candlelight effects of the rooms, resulting in an "up-lit" effect of a Watteau painting. For all its dramatic invention, however, the premise of the exhibition was to establish an apparent discourse between objects. In every room furniture remained as originally placed or was only slightly shifted to accommodate the mannequins. The actions of the figures were, therefore, directly predicated on concepts originating from the rooms and the décor.

Eighteenth-century prints, drawings, and paintings documenting the insouciant life of the ancien régime elite served as inspiration for the vignettes, as did popular libertine literature of the period. In particular, the curators were reliant on two works for establishing the exhibition's narrative parameters. The first, Jean-François Bastide's novella *La Petite Maison* (1758), linked architecture and decorative arts to stratagems of seduction, while the second, Jean-Michel Moreau le Jeune's compilation of engravings, *Monument du costume* (1789), described aristocratic diversions with idealized "day-in-the-life-of" detail.

La Petite Maison is, as the architectural scholar Rodolphe El-Khoury has written, "an intersection of the libertine novel and critical commentary on architecture." For Bastide's hero, the Marquis de Trémicour, a worldly counterpart to the better-known Vicomte de Valmont in Choderlos de Laclos's *Les Liaisons dangereuses* (1782), the sumptuous aesthetic of eighteenth-century French design is less simple scenography than an active accomplice in his amorous pursuits. For example, a particularly challenging interlude for Mélite, the elusive subject of the marquis's attentions, occurs when she is led into an ingeniously decorated round salon, similar spatially to the Museum's own Bordeaux Room (p. 99). Anthropomorphism insinuates itself when the salon emerges as a third party, and, in effect, as a seducer even more compelling than (though in the service of) the ardent marquis. In the world of de Trémicour and Mélite, erotic games are played out by extravagantly dressed elites in homes of luxurious refinement.

While the dress of the two protagonists is not described, de Trémicour would have worn a sleekly fitted silk suit embellished with lace jabot and cuffs, while Mélite was probably attired in a *robe à la française* of the type seen on page 49. Her natural silhouette would have been exaggerated by her corset and panniers, the one constraining her body as the other amplified its effect. The finely embellished, elaborately brocaded silk comprising her dress would have been arranged to display the finer points of her exposed nape and bust. At the same time, it would have highlighted the grace with which she could negotiate its sheer volume, whether her full skirt through a doorway and around a delicately poised table or her lace cuffs, or *engageantes,* above a fragile tea service or a pot of rouge.

As Mimi Hellman describes in her essay, this interaction of the body with objects was a carefully choreographed, challenging exercise with important implications of status and social refinement. While in some instances in "Dangerous Liaisons" specific pieces of furniture inspired the telling actions of the figures, in others the rooms and their history precipitated the narratives. Because of the aesthetic unity that characterized the various arts presented, whether in terms of styles, motives, or technical accomplishments, fortuitous correspondences transpired. The transformative silhouette of an informal gown juxtaposed with a mechanical table, or the inflated hairstyle of a woman at her dressing table in a room with Jacob chairs with balloon finials, associate disparate phenomena into a legible gestalt.

In the exhibition Kinmonth referenced dressmaker's forms when he covered the mannequins with fine linen, an act that also recalled the interior finishes of eighteenth-century corsets. While clearly dummies, the figures were posed in naturalistic postures derived from period paintings and prints. The positioning of mannequins in attitudes of the eighteenth century resulted in a convincing representation of elite decorum. For example, the female figures were not bent at the waist because a woman fitted with a corset and center-front busk was precluded from doing so. Instead, the eighteenth-century *femme du monde* was compelled to lean over with her back rigid, bending at her hips as in the case of the woman hovering over the prostrate figure in the Varengeville Room (p. 65). The wigs, made from hand-knotted human hair and designed by Campbell Young and his colleague, Chris Redman, introduced a particularly convincing visual effect, especially when they were powdered. A subtle detail seen in portraits of the period emerged more vividly when the powder drifted down to the roots and scalp, creating a delicate *sfumato,* lighter along the crown and hairline, and darker at the sides and back of the head. The exhibition's powdered coiffures balanced the lush luster and volume of the costumes of the day. With such attention to detail, the allure of the eighteenth-century woman was poetically evoked.

La Petite Maison concludes with Mélite emotionally overcome by the beauty of the décor in de Trémicour's house. While there was always the possibility that the placement of mannequins in the luxurious hauteur of The Wrightsman Galleries might fail to communicate the highly evolved sensibilities of the period, any doubts as to the validity of the project vanished when the figures began to be positioned in the rooms. With their opulent costumes, the mannequins humanized the scale of even the grandest space, and the narratives engaged the forms and design details of the Metropolitan's formidable masterworks of furniture and decorative arts with a compelling aesthetic unity. As demonstrated in the exhibition and in this lavishly illustrated publication, the exquisite *art de vivre* of eighteenth-century France, expressed through the dangerously seductive liaison of fashion and furniture, still has the power to please the mind and overwhelm the senses.

INTERIOR MOTIVES: SEDUCTION BY DECORATION
IN EIGHTEENTH-CENTURY FRANCE

MIMI HELLMAN

"I was very curious: it was no longer Madame de T—— that I desired, but her cabinet."

Dominique Vivant Denon, *No Tomorrow* (1777)

Imagine a seduction in which the principal object of desire is not the body of the beloved, but rather the room in which the play of invitation and capitulation unfolds. Imagine a seduction in which every move is shaped by a piece of furniture. Imagine a seduction in which pleasure is offered and denied without the removal of single piece of clothing. Welcome to the decorated interior in eighteenth-century France.

The vignettes of *Dangerous Liaisons* vividly suggest some of the ways in which the design of clothing and interiors worked together to create elegant environments for intimate encounters. The narratives of seduction focus largely on interactions between people inspired by libertine imagery and literature: the flirtatious gesture, the stolen caress, the gorgeously attired bodies displayed and enjoyed with varying degrees of propriety. These scenarios offer a provocative point of departure for thinking about the interpersonal dynamics of the decorated interior. While it is difficult to assess the degree to which libertine sensibilities corresponded with actual practice, many social encounters were indeed conceived as rarefied rituals of seduction. Moreover, the intimacies of the interior played out not only between people but also between people and the furniture that surrounded them. Objects such as chairs and tables were active protagonists in an elaborate game of cultivated sociability. Through their luxurious materials and strategically designed forms, they facilitated a process of alluring self-presentation and elegant communication that was central to the formation of elite identities. At the same time, however, the effective use of furniture presented certain challenges that, if not met gracefully, could seriously compromise a person's social seductiveness. In other words the dangerous liaisons of the eighteenth-century interior involved not only tantalizing bodies but also tantalizing objects. Welcome to a world where, as suggested by the protagonist of

Dominique Vivant Denon's novella *No Tomorrow*, a woman's private study (*cabinet*) could be even more seductive than the woman herself.

Elite social interaction in eighteenth-century France took place in densely decorated interiors filled with diverse objects crafted from a wide range of materials. Walls were covered with carved paneling, textiles, and mirrors, while floors gleamed with polished parquet. Furnishings included silk-upholstered chairs with carved and gilded frames, tables and cabinets veneered with exotic wood and lacquer, and a multitude of fittings from gilded-bronze light fixtures to brilliantly glazed porcelain vases. Many of these objects were highly specialized, designed to be used for leisure activities such as conversation, reading, letter writing, handwork, dining, and game playing. Such pursuits might seem trivial from a modern perspective, but for eighteenth-century elites they were important means of self-definition. Physical labor and preoccupations with economic gain and professional achievement were considered incompatible with a noble heritage and high status. Therefore the most powerful way to demonstrate social superiority was to pursue a life of leisure, luxury, and refinement. To be elite was to turn everyday existence into an elaborate rejection of physical effort and base human needs. To be elite was to transform oneself into a living work of art. And the decorated interior was the principal arena in which this performance of privilege was staged.

The material abundance and social uses of the interior are exemplified by images such as Jean-François de Troy's *The Reading from Molière* of about 1728 and an engraving of 1781 after Jean-Michel Moreau le Jeune. In de Troy's painting (p. 14), a convivial group of men and women gathers near a fireplace, sheltered from drafts by a folding screen. A man seated at the center looks up from a book he has been reading aloud and is caught up in a web of glances—both reciprocated and unreciprocated—that binds the group together. Two of the women (one standing at center and another seated to the right) seem to look directly out of the picture as if acknowledging our presence and inviting us to join the party.

Contributing significantly to the scene's sense of intimacy are the design and position of the chairs. With their low, wide seats, tilted backs, and generously stuffed upholstery, they seem to invite hours of relaxed comfort. Their arrangement in a tight cluster brings the elegantly dressed bodies close together, the women's skirts overlapping in a sumptuous heap of fabrics. These chairs exemplify the specialization that characterized eighteenth-century French furniture. They are ideally suited to an informal gathering for reading and conversation but would not have been used for other kinds of activities. A hairdressing chair, for example, would have a low back to facilitate the process of combing, curling, and powdering, and its seat might revolve for further convenience. A writing chair would have minimal arms, to allow it to be drawn close to a desk, and its supports would be positioned beneath the center of each side of the seat, rather than at the corners, to accommodate the weight and posture of someone leaning forward with legs apart.

The engraving after Moreau le Jeune (p. 18) further suggests this fascination with customized design and its contribution to social intimacy. Two couples are engaging in a flirtatious supper party. One woman pours wine for an eager-looking man, while the other teases her companion by holding a piece of paper—perhaps a love letter from another admirer—just beyond his grasp. Like the women in de Troy's painting, she includes the viewer in the fun by looking out of the picture with a coy, sidelong gaze.

Here, too, the furniture and other objects do much to facilitate personal encounters. The dining table is just large enough for four, and the trim lines of the chairs allow bodies to lean close together.

The dining table, draped in linen and strewn with a companionable clutter of plates and utensils, is flanked by two smaller tables that are much more specialized in design. Compact, easily moved, and fitted with shelves and compartments, they are meant to keep items such as wine bottles, dishes, and napkins within easy reach. Dining practice developed many refinements during the eighteenth century, including serving wine from chilled containers and providing each diner with his or her own wineglass, which was rinsed between refills. The side tables in the engraving include wells for cooling bottles, and the one in the foreground holds a scallop-rimmed basin in which upturned stemware awaits the next round of drinks. By making it possible for diners to serve themselves, these design features reduced the need for servants and allowed meals to become far more private and informal affairs. The image vividly suggests the erotic turn that this social intimacy could take as diners attended to each other's appetites, gastronomic and otherwise.

The eighteenth-century interior, then, was a highly articulated landscape in which numerous, diverse objects enhanced the pursuit of leisure. This design sophistication was widely regarded as uniquely modern and uniquely French, a sensitivity to personal comfort and convenience that existed in no other place or time. And, indeed, many eighteenth-century objects do seem to be tremendously accommodating, easy and pleasurable to use and perfectly tailored to dynamics of elite social life. There was, however, a catch. To yield up an enjoyable experience, furniture had to be used properly, and this was not as obvious or simple as it might at first seem. To understand how elite individuals inhabited their elegant environments, we need to know more about how they were expected to conduct themselves and what it took to achieve an ideal social persona. The delights of the interior came at a price—one that only a privileged few could pay.

The central premise of elite social behavior was that the body was an instrument of pleasure. Interaction was conceived as a process of seduction—not necessarily a pursuit of overt sexual expression, but rather an exchange in which individuals sought to engage and delight each other with an artfully conducted repertoire of pleasing poses, gestures, expressions, and conversation. The goal was to use physical appearance and communication skills to gratify the aesthetic and social sensibilities of others, while at the same time demonstrating reciprocal pleasure in response to similar efforts on their part. This was no easy matter—social seduction was a delicate balancing act fraught with paradox. It meant avoiding the equally displeasing extremes of aggression and impassivity. It meant being well groomed but not self-absorbed. It meant pleasing others, and being pleased by them, without seeming to be pleased with oneself. Moreover, this cycle of mutual pleasing was to be conducted in a way that seemed utterly natural, as if agreeable manners were innate rather than learned. Conduct that betrayed effort and awkwardness suggested a worker's lack of cultivation or the laboriously acquired pretentions of a newly wealthy bourgeois. The best way to suggest long-standing social privilege was to seduce, and be seduced, with an acute self-awareness masquerading as selfless ease.

The mandate of pleasure governed every aspect of elite behavior. For example, the socially adept individual demonstrated a bearing that was upright but not stiff, self-contained yet relaxed. Physical motion should be smooth and flowing, neither too rapid nor too slow. Gestures should be expressive without being too broad, abrupt, or agitated. Similarly, facial expression should be animated without succumbing to such offenses as grinning, frowning, or staring. Any semblance of confrontation should be avoided: one should never stand directly in front of another person, grasp their sleeve to get attention, or stamp a foot for emphasis. In conversation, speech should be modulated in tone, pedantic subjects avoided, and personal interests forsaken for those of others. It was considered

rude to make long speeches or blunt statements, and preferable to communicate through the more subtle, indirect tactics of euphemism and qualification.

But it was not enough to observe the same general code of conduct in all social situations. Every set of circumstances demanded behavior that was tailored to the gender, rank, and marital status of one's interlocutor and the location, time of day, and occasion of the encounter. For example, a young, unmarried count would approach a widowed duchess at a formal ball in a way that was very different from his overtures to an unmarried woman during a garden stroll or his conversation with a gentleman of equal rank at a game table in a private residence. A broad smile that was companionable at the game table might be considered disrespectful at the ball and positively lewd in the garden. The cultivated individual was thus required to maintain a constant state of social vigilance—surveying shifting circumstances, assessing relevant variables, and adapting actions accordingly.

This, then, was the code of conduct that shaped encounters within the decorated interior. The body was used in ways that suppressed its most basic qualities—its awkwardness, its weightiness, its spontaneous impulses—in order to deliver a pleasing performance of grace and ease. In this context furniture design takes on a whole new look. Consider once again the scenario presented by de Troy (p. 14). The low chairs, with their sloping backs and soft cushions, would be difficult to sink into and arise from with fluid ease. Accomplished successfully, such movements could highlight a person's physical grace and provide opportunities for enjoyable interaction as, say, a gentleman offers a lady his hand for support. But accomplished awkwardly, the act of sitting or standing could expose the imperfections of an ungainly body or an ill-calculated attempt at gallantry. Moreover, once ensconced, the sitter is subjected to further conditions. The chair's high, broad back frames the head and upper body, drawing attention to facial expressions and hand gestures in a way that could either enhance allure or make gracelessness all the more apparent. And, if several such chairs are arranged in a tight cluster, as in de Troy's painting, their occupants are effectively immobilized by their proximity and so visible to one another that no movement would go unnoticed. The ultimate effect of this arrangement is precisely the opposite of what the chair seems designed to do—it may invite the user to loll with abandon, but it poses major social risks to those who dare to do so.

Similarly, the engraving of the supper party (p. 18) is as full of dangers as it is of delights. Consider how many objects there are to bump into, tip over, or break: the lightweight chairs and side tables, the fragile wineglasses slippery from their bath of cool water, the generously draped tablecloth just waiting to catch in the heel of a shoe. On the other hand, consider the opportunities for pleasurable performance that are offered by the very same objects. The well-stocked side tables might inspire a gentleman to offer his companion a napkin, opening it with a flourish and moving a little closer to her in the process. The act of rinsing, filling, and drinking from a wineglass might enable a woman to show off the graceful tilt of her head, the delicacy of her hands, the rosiness of her lips. The more objects that were involved in a social scenario, the greater the potential for both accident and enjoyment. The art of interaction meant negotiating a decorative minefield while seeming utterly at ease.

The vignettes of *Dangerous Liaisons* are full of such promising yet precarious moments. In "The Card Game" (pp. 102–3), the gaming table is simultaneously convenient and challenging. It has a light, compact, folding structure that makes it easy to position and reposition according to the changing inclinations of the players. Gathered around the table's small surface, several people are brought together in intimate proximity. But imagine how easily elbows or knees could collide with a jolt rather than a teasing nudge. Imagine how an abrupt gesture of triumph or concession could make a teacup fall to the floor, or how someone departing too quickly—especially a woman in voluminous skirts—could overturn the entire thing.

Similarly, the specialized chair used by one man to watch the game both flatters the body and demands a significant measure of self-control. Termed a *voyeuse* (literally, a "viewer"), it is designed to be straddled backward by a man (others were made to be knelt upon by a woman). The saddle-shaped seat accommodates the user's parted legs, sheathed in tight breeches, and the padded top rail offers a comfortable resting place for the forearms. Successfully used, it would have produced a pleasing pose, with the man's limbs elegantly extended in a way that highlighted his lace cuffs and well-formed calves. At the same time, the proper way to occupy such a chair may not have been obvious to everyone, and it demands a physical dexterity that does not come easily to all. Thus the *voyeuse*, like many other objects, yields pleasure—for user and observer alike—only if its image-enhancing design features are gracefully engaged. It is also a remarkable example of the way in which eighteenth-century furniture turned even the most seemingly simple activity into an artful spectacle. The casual act of sitting backward, which easily could be done with a standard side chair, becomes an elaborately choreographed pose. The chair is a pedestal for the body, displaying it for the delectation of others, while the sitter, in keeping with the rules of cultivated conduct, appears unaware of his allure.

The social power of furniture is perhaps most vividly demonstrated in the vignette entitled "The Levée" (pp. 38–39). It represents a widely practiced eighteenth-century ritual, also known as the toilette, in which elite women (and many men) received visitors while dressing. As suggested by an engraving after Nicolas Lavreince II (p. 21), the toilette was a semipublic event in which an individual presided over the construction of his or her appearance while conducting a variety of interactions with a steady stream of visitors. These might include both casual and intimate acquaintances, household staff, tailors or milliners in the process of completing commissions, artists or writers in search of patronage, and sellers of a wide range of luxury goods from dress trimmings to freshly brewed coffee. And although grooming and conversation were the central activities, the event also incorporated other leisure pursuits such as serving refreshments and reading aloud.

Numerous eighteenth-century images and texts represent the toilette as an event devoted solely to female vanity, frivolity, and sexual machinations. But it was also an important occasion for the game of social seduction through which elite identities were defined. Virtually every aspect of the ritual's dynamics—spatial, temporal, material, and behavioral—provided the protagonist with an opportunity to express both her own social standing and those of others. Through wide-ranging conversation and the display of personal possessions—from books to jewelry to perfume—it provided numerous opportunities to demonstrate wealth and taste, exchange information, and develop relationships. Moreover, by controlling the point at which visitors were received, the duration of their stay, and the way in which they were allowed—or not allowed—to engage with objects and events, a woman at her toilette could communicate very specific degrees of social intimacy or distance. For instance, an old friend might be admitted alone, while her hostess was still bare of makeup, and invited to sit close to the dressing table and drink some rich, expensive chocolate from a newly acquired cup. In contrast, a creditor might be summoned to a roomful of people during the final stages of the dressing process and made to wait, standing by the door, before being dismissed without payment, let alone refreshment. In both cases the visitor would know exactly where she or he stood in the nuanced hierarchy of favor. The toilette, in other words, was an

early modern version of networking—a strategic cultivation of interpersonal connections that define and strengthen social positions.

More than any other elite social ritual, the toilette centered on the aesthetic and social seductiveness of the body. In the engraving after Lavreince a woman has her hair done while examining fabric samples and entertaining a clergyman and a musician. Several visual cues hint at some kind of erotic intrigue. The clergyman fixes his hostess with a satisfied stare while clutching the top of a rather phallic cane. And while the musician's face is invisible, the broken strings erupting from the top of his instrument suggest that he, too, may be in a somewhat flustered state. But the focal point of the composition is the woman herself. Turning away from her dressing table, she gestures toward a length of fabric in a way that simultaneously asserts her authority as a consumer and displays her bodily charms. The simple act of pointing becomes an occasion for displaying an elegantly extended arm and allowing her breasts to be revealed, as if by accident, between the ruffled edges of her parted robe. This is a quintessential example of the artful innocence with which the elite individual was expected to make herself pleasing to others. By attending momentarily to something other than her appearance, she actually draws attention to it, inviting delectation without crossing the line into overt exhibitionism. Indeed the title of the print ("What does the abbé think of it?") is a play on this feint: she is asking the clergyman about the piece of cloth, but his eyes are fixed on her chest.

Yet the delights of the toilette were every bit as qualified as those of other leisure activities. In fact it probably posed more challenges than any other social event, for its extensive array of furniture and accessories offered almost endless opportunities to either showcase virtuosity or betray a lack of finesse. Many of these objects were small, intricately designed, and liable to spill or break. There were cosmetics to be applied with tiny brushes, beverages to be served in thin porcelain cups, slippery ribbons to be retrieved from lidded boxes—all, of course, while conversing amiably with visitors and betraying no sign of awkwardness or effort.

The accessories of the toilette were often arranged, as in the engraving after Lavreince, on a plain table draped with fabric and lace. But the ritual achieved its greatest opportunities and difficulties when it was conducted with a specialized dressing table such as the one featured in "The Levée." This piece is designed to be manipulated in a variety of ways in order to serve multiple functions. The upper half has two lidded storage compartments, an adjustable reading stand that rotates in its frame to reveal a mirror on the other side, and a drawer fitted with an inkstand and covered by a hinged lid that can be used as a writing surface. This entire top section can be removed, revealing four short legs, and used by someone propped up in bed. The lower half of the table incorporates two writing slides at front and back and two deep side drawers divided into compartments. And to complete its attractions, it is equipped with various objects for grooming, sewing, and eating—including rock-crystal perfume flasks, a tortoiseshell eyelash comb, a lacquer needle case, and a breakfast set of Sèvres porcelain.

Dressing tables like this were veritable arsenals for social seduction. Each manipulation of the object and its fittings would have involved a particular pose or gestural sequence on the part of the user. Opening the hinged lids of the upper section might show off the turn of the arms, while bending to retrieve something from a lower compartment might allow a glimpse of a powdered neck or barely contained breast. On the other hand, consider the awkwardness of groping for the button that makes the mirror revolve, or allowing a drooping sleeve to sweep an ink bottle off the writing slide. Once again, the object seems endlessly accommodating but elicits a pleasing performance only if the user knows how it works and remains in control of the process.

It should be clear by now that social seduction in eighteenth-century France was impossible without furniture. Objects were like extensions of the body, part of a wardrobe that, correctly worn, could turn the activities of elite existence into dances of artful persuasion. The wardrobe analogy is really very apt, for the way in which furniture simultaneously valorized the body and controlled its conduct is closely related to the aesthetic and social impact of clothing. Lace cuffs, for instance, emphasized smooth, soft hands that were never subjected to manual labor. Shoes with high heels and elongated toes made the wearer seem to hover above the floor and encouraged a light tiptoeing gait. Men's coats were cut to curve away from the front of the body, conveying an impression of flowing, forward-tilted movement. A similar effect was produced in women by skirts that were fuller in the back than in the front and corsets that flattened the abdomen and pushed the chest forward. The elite body was thus doubly disciplined by fashion, shaped by both its decorative dressing and its decorated environment.

At first glance the lavishly staged tableaux of *Dangerous Liaisons* might seem to exemplify a world of pure elegance. But the real revelation is the way in which they suggest the risks of pleasure. The seductions of the eighteenth-century interior unfolded amid the possibility—indeed, the likelihood—of numerous unseductive entanglements. Interacting with decorated spaces was in itself a dangerous liaison: an encounter spurred by attraction and fraught with uncertainty, part savvy calculation and part unpredictable effect, the magnitude of its dangers equal only to the scope of its delights. Like teasing lovers, objects were both alluring and resistant, promising infinite rewards even as they posed one challenge after another. And, once we begin to understand the workings of these interior motives, the figures who animate the vignettes, like those who look out at us from de Troy's convivial reading circle (p. 14) or Moreau le Jeune's intimate supper (p. 18), become even more suggestive. They seem to take on a knowing, conspiratorial air—poised for our admiration, inviting us to join the game, daring us to take a seat.

THE PORTRAIT: AN UNEXPECTED ENTANGLEMENT
DE TESSÉ ROOM (PARIS, CA. 1768–72)

The writer William Combe began his *Poetical Epistle to Sir Joshua Reynolds* (1777) with the observation "This seems to be a Portrait-painting Age." Whether, as Combe avowed, it was owing to "the increase of Sentiment" and "the spirit of Luxury which pervades all ranks and professions of men," Europe in the eighteenth century witnessed an escalation and heightened appreciation of fashionable portraiture. In France some of the most famous painters of the period were women, such as Adélaïde Labille-Guiard, Élisabeth Vigée-Lebrun, and Rose Adélaïde Ducreux, whose superlative *Self-Portrait with a Harp* (ca. 1790, p. 47) dominates the De Tessé Room. All of these artists achieved notoriety through their depictions of society women, none more so than Vigée-Lebrun, whose ability to please and flatter her female sitters made her one of the most sought-after portraitists not only in France but throughout Europe. Known for her soft, subdued palette, she painted such notable women as Madame du Barry, Madame de Staël, and the duchesse de Polignac, but she is best known for her portraits of Marie-Antoinette, whom she first painted in 1778. Gradually becoming the queen's official portraitist, or *portraitiste en titre*, Vigée-Lebrun was admitted to the Académie Royale de Peinture et de Sculpture in 1783 (along with her rival Labille-Guiard), allowing her to participate in the biennial Salon at the Louvre.

As a tribute to Vigée-Lebrun and her contemporaries, the De Tessé Room reveals several conventions of eighteenth-century portraiture. Typically, the painter is shown with palette and brushes in hand and canvas hidden from view, as in Labille-Guiard's *Self-Portrait with Two Pupils* (1785, p. 24). While both the artist and the sitter in the room are dressed *à la mode,* there is a clear distinction in their appearance. The artist wears the *robe retroussée dans les poches,* a style in which the skirt was pulled out from the side pockets of the dress and draped over the back. Derived from the wardrobe of workingwomen, this casual, practical fashion was adopted by the nobility in the 1770s, when the English custom of walking in the countryside became popular among the French aristocracy. The sitter, in contrast, wears the *robe à l'anglaise,* a style that was first seen in France in the middle of the century and reappeared in the 1780s through the influence of Anglomania. Consisting of a back-fitted, front-closing robe and petticoat, the robe, at this date, was worn with a small, curved pannier (although, sometimes, it attained its round, billowing silhouette through the drapes of the skirt alone). Versatile enough for informal and semiformal settings, the style is also worn by the sitter's friend, whose sweetly innocent pink-and-white-striped robe, a candy-colored version of the gown represented in Rose Adélaïde Ducreux's *Self-Portrait with a Harp* belies her worldly, flirtatious entanglement with the sitter's husband.

In the eighteenth century the main function of fashion in portraiture was to bestow upon the sitter a sense of eternal beauty and elegance. The sitter's white muslin *robe à l'anglaise* conveys this conceit less by its design than by its fabric, which suggests a Claudeian pastoralism. Cotton emerged as a modish material in the 1770s and was promoted by such fashion leaders as Marie-Antoinette, who, in the summer, often wore a white muslin gown in the style of a chemise. In a sartorial expression of Jean-Jacques Rousseau's "back-to-nature" philosophy, the queen acted out Arcadian pursuits in this simple chemise *à la jardinière* or *en belle fermière* at her idealized peasant cottage, Le Hameau de la Reine, at the Petit Trianon at Versailles. This rusticized raiment, based on the simple tubes of white muslin worn by Creole women, was sported by the queen for the portrait attributed to Vigée-Lebrun (herself an advocate of pastoral costume) that was shown in the Salon of 1783 (p. 8). Deemed unsuitable for a queen of France, the painting had to be withdrawn, but the attendant excitement helped to popularize the style among women of fashion. Typical of the eighteenth-century practice of naming styles of dress after social types, the costume, which presaged the Neoclassical fashions of the 1790s and early 1800s (and was itself an expression of classicism), came to be known as the *chemise à la reine* as early as the mid-1770s. This practice extended to furniture, as seen in the carved-and-gilded daybed, or *duchesse en bateau*, on which the sitter is reclining. Apart from her stays, aristocratic principles of etiquette and deportment account for her rigid, unrelaxed demeanor. Made by Jean-Baptiste II Lelarge, the daybed has a detachable footrest, tailoring repose to the length or position of the individual. Designed to shape and cradle the user, the daybed was intended to enhance comfort and informality, while displaying the body to best advantage.

An oriental as well as a pastoral sensibility is expressed by the sitter's choice of fabric, which, like many cottons from the period, was imported from India. The robe bears a Sanskrit inscription woven into the selvedge. Like pastoralism, orientalism was a convention of portraiture intended to evoke a sense of timelessness. Men often posed in a dressing gown to indicate their literary and philosophical predilections, as seen in Louis-Michel van Loo's portrait of Denis Diderot (1767, p. 27). Frequently styled after the Japanese kimono, it could be made from a variety of materials, including Indian chintz (such a gown was known in France as the *robe de chambre d'indienne*). A popular form of undress, or *déshabillé*, the dressing gown was also acceptable apparel in which to receive visitors. The version worn by the sitter's faithless husband in the De Tessé Room is made from silk, the elegant pattern of which finds a visual counterpart in the intricate silver-thread embroidery of his wife's *robe à l'anglaise*. In a tangible expression of the synergy between eighteenth-century fashion and furniture, the pattern extends to the graceful latticework marquetry of the *table mécanique*, which occupies a central position in the room. This table, which could be used for eating, reading, writing, and dressing was made by the royal cabinetmaker Jean-Henri Riesener for Marie-Antoinette's apartment at Versailles and was intended for her amusement at the time of the birth of her first child, Marie-Thérèse Charlotte.

THE LEVÉE: THE ASSIDUOUS ADMIRER
CABRIS ROOM (GRASSE, CA. 1775–78)

In the eighteenth century the morning toilette merged private ritual with public performance. It was an occasion for women of fashion not only to receive friends and keep abreast of the latest news and gossip but also to transact business. For Madame de Pompadour, the *levée* (one of the few times that she was not obliged to follow the finer points of court etiquette) was a means of securing and furthering her own status at Versailles, as well as that of others. In his portrait of Madame de Pompadour at her dressing table (1758 p. 37), François Boucher alludes to the fact that the *levée* was a site of power for the royal mistress by placing the image of Louis XV on a cameo bracelet, which she wears on her right wrist. It is thought that the portrait is based on an engraving executed by Pompadour herself, a potent symbol of her influence over the king. The ambitious courtier, the duc de Croy, realized that if he were to secure Pompadour's goodwill, and, in turn, advance his position, he would need to be a regular attendee at her toilette. In his memoirs he noted how even the more powerful courtiers competed with one another for an invitation to this most private of rituals. For many women, however, the privacy of their cabinet de toilette provided an opportunity for romantic intrigues. Louis-Roland Trinquesse explored the amorous machinations of the morning toilette in his *Interior Scene with Two Women and a Gentleman* (1776, detail p. 34), which depicts a suitor appealing to the heart and emotions of a young woman as she attends to her coiffure with an air of self-conscious nonchalance. Women well versed in the art of dressing relished the vanities and coquetries of the toilette. As the *Petit Dictionnaire de la cour* (1788) noted, "A charming woman uses more subtlety and politics in her dressing than there are in all the governments of Europe."

Referencing such *tableaux de mode* as Trinquesse's *Interior Scene*, the Cabris Room's mise-en-scène captures the intimate social intercourse of the morning toilette. With bright, midday sunlight streaming through the windows (eleven-thirty being the usual time that women of leisure began accepting visitors), the woman of the house wears typical toilette costume of underwear (stays and a chemise) and negligee garments (a peignoir). She is seated in a hairdressing chair, or *fauteuil à coiffer*, the low back of which was designed to facilitate the styling process and draw attention to a woman's neck and shoulders. Her admirer is dressed in a silk faille suit or, *habit à la française,* customarily comprising coat, breeches, and waistcoat. While it suggests a faintly démodé sensibility through its cut, cuffs, and collar, the suit of silk moiré worn by the hairdresser is the height of fashion. As Philippe Séguy observes in *The Age of Napoleon* (1989), hairdressers were prominent figures in elite society during the eighteenth century. The court was both amused and irritated by the erratic behavior and astonishing arrogance of Marie-Antoinette's coiffeur, Léonard. It was Léonard who created the famous *coiffure à l'enfant* for the queen, who, after the birth of her second son, Louis Charles, suffered severe hair loss.

From the 1770s hairstyles increased in height and complexity, becoming the source of endless satire. Specialized publications recorded this creative effervescence, such as Legros de Rumigny's *L'Art de la coëffure des dames françoises, avec des estampes, où sont représentées les têtes coëffées* (1767–70), a volume of which rests on a side chair in the Cabris Room. Strewn on the floor are cards depicting women in fashionable coiffures. Used to play a popular Dutch lottery game of the period, they provide insight into the range and diversity of hairstyles in late eighteenth-century Europe. Subject to the whims of the moment, styles were often named after events, objects, and even people. The *coiffure à la Montgolfier*, for instance, received its appellation from the inventors of the hot-air balloon. In June 1783 the Montgolfier brothers made the first public demonstration of a model hot-air balloon, and on September 19, 1783, they launched a balloon carrying a duck, sheep, and a cockerel from Versailles in the presence of Louis XVI and Marie-Antoinette. The style sported by the woman in the Cabris Room is the *coiffure à la Charlière*, named after the hydrogen balloon invented by Jacques Charles. On December 1, 1783, Charles (along with Marie-Noël Robert) ascended in *La Charlière* to a height of 1,800 feet over the Tuileries. This event inspired the side chair, or *chaise à la reine*, on which the woman's admirer is seated. One of a pair, it was made by Georges Jacob for Marie-Antoinette's boudoir in the Château de Tuileries and reveals such details as spherical finials based on the roundness of a hydrogen balloon (as opposed to the more pear-shaped hot-air balloon).

Draped over the auxiliary *chaise à la reine* is a *robe à la polonaise*, a style that became popular from the mid-1770s. Worn over a petticoat that reached just above the ankles, the *polonaise* was cut like the *robe à l'anglaise* (but worn over a bustle, which was less restrictive than a pannier and served to accentuate the hollow of the back). At the back a system of cord pulleys allowed three panels of the dress (a tail and two wings) to be raised so that they fell in curves over the petticoat to create airy poufs of material. Like the *coiffure à la Charlière*, the *robe à la polonaise*, whose playfully inflated silhouette continues the Cabris Room's ballooning iconography, claims cultural significance. The first partition of Poland, dividing it among Austria, Prussia, and Russia, took place in 1772, and it is said that the robe derives its name from this event. Through its system of transformative drawstrings, the *polonaise* could be worn in a variety of different styles (although the tail and two wings was the most common). In the Cabris Room this mutability finds a corollary with the traveling table, or *table de voyage*. Made by Martin Carlin, the table could be manipulated to reveal a mirror, several drawers and compartments, and eating, reading, writing, and dressing surfaces. Often such a table was the focal point of a woman's morning toilette, designed, as it was, to reveal her ease and grace. Incorporating two separable elements that could be used individually or in combination, the table required acute physical dexterity. A woman's skillful manipulation of her *table de voyage* demonstrated her gestural virtuosity, offering an opportunity for seductive and coquettish behavior that imbued the whole ritual of dressing with a potent erotic receptivity.

THE MUSIC LESSON: A WINDOW OF OPPORTUNITY
PAAR ROOM (VIENNA, CA. 1765–71)

Music was central to the concept and practice of artful living in the eighteenth century. Shaping the rhythm of quotidian aristocratic experience, music, or rather music appreciation, was not only a leisure activity in itself, pursued at the opera, ballet, and concert, but it was also an adjunct to other leisure activities, animating private dinners, garden parties, and salon gatherings. Like music appreciation, musical proficiency, especially in women, was an essential component in the formation of elite social personae. John Essex in *The Young Ladies Conduct: or, Rules for Education, Under Several Heads* (1722) wrote that music "is certainly a very great Accomplishment to the LADIES; it refines the Taste, polishes the Mind; and is an Entertainment, without other Views, that preserves them from the Rust of Idleness, that most pernicious Enemy to Virtue." While intended for a British audience, Essex's musings on the benefits of a musical education for women applied equally to the French (although they may have been less receptive to his moralizing overtones). In France, as in England, musical aptitude was seen as a sign of refined femininity, greatly enhancing a young woman's marriage prospects. Parents went to great lengths to secure the most skillful teachers for their daughters' educations. Since most teachers were men, however, this education frequently extended beyond the musical to the sensual. Indeed, music masters, or *maîtres de musique*, were often seen as carnal creatures that preyed upon a young woman's latent sexuality.

The Paar Room takes the theme of the music lesson as an occasion for sexual transgression, a theme familiar to readers of libertine literature in the eighteenth century. In Choderlos de Laclos's *Les Liaisons dangereuses* (1782), the music lesson provides the callow Chevalier Danceny with an opportunity to seduce the weak-willed, convent-educated "rosebud" Cécile Volanges. Writing to her old school friend Sophie Carnay, Cécile enthuses, "I spend a lot of time practicing my singing and harp, and I'm enjoying them more now I haven't got a teacher or rather because I've got a better one [Danceny]." Of all musical instruments associated with women, and, indeed, culturally sanctioned, the harp was viewed as especially apposite for young women (unlike the flute, which was a potent symbol of male sexuality). Marie-Antoinette, who, in 1773, wrote in a letter to her mother that she was always loyal to her harp and took a long lesson every day, helped to popularize the harp among women of fashion. Philip Joseph Hinner, *maître de harpe de la reine,* dedicated several harp sonatas to the dauphine including "Haughtiness" and "The Chatterer," titles that evoke the harp's ability to project a player's coquetry. In the hands of a voluptuary the harp was a powerful instrument of seduction, as exemplified in Jean-Michel Moreau le Jeune's *L'Accord parfait* (1777, p. 44), which shows a skilled musician plucking the harp strings and heartstrings of two admiring gallants. The harp, however, was a sexual stimulant for players as well as spectators. Necessitating an intrusion between the legs, the harp became an effective autoerotic apparatus.

As seen in the Paar Room and Moreau Le Jeune's etching, the harp allowed a woman to reveal her musical virtuosity as well as to display her pretty hands and nimble fingers. The pedal harp, played by the student in the Paar Room, also enabled her to show off a delicate foot and a "well-turned ankle." Apparently invented by Jacob Hochbrucker in Bavaria at the turn of the eighteenth century, the pedal harp found its greatest success in Paris, where, in the last quarter of the century, it was taken up by elite women. Pedal harps were, in themselves, exquisite works of art. Used as "props" in portraiture, they denoted status, taste, and a highly refined fashionability, as in Rose Adélaïde Ducreux's *Self-Portrait with a Harp* (p. 47). The harp in the Paar Room was made by Renault et Chatelain and is sumptuously ornamented in the Rococo style that infuses the room's boiserie and furniture. Revealing gilt carvings on the neck, column, and pedestal, its soundboard is hand-painted with floral and musical motifs and chinoiserie. This oriental aesthetic extends to the student's *robe à la française,* an open-front, back-pleated dress worn with a matching petticoat and stomacher (a panel with a V- or U-shaped bottom that usually covered the stays and was attached to the robe with pins). Made from Chinese-export damask, its sober color is offset by its striped lining (a design "secret" reserved for its wearer and her intimates). Exoticism defines the adjustable music stand, which could also be used for reading and writing and could be adjusted to the height of the user. Executed in Brazilian tulipwood, its graining imitates the *changeant* taffeta of the Italian music tutor's *habit à la française.* As Richard Leppert argues in *Music and Image* (1998), Italian teachers, while victims of ridicule and condescension because of their status as "aliens," were highly sought-after in France and England in the eighteenth century. Perhaps the most explicit display of exoticism, however, is the voyeur's *robe à la française* of *chine à la branche,* with its distinctive water-blotting pattern (achieved by printing the pattern onto the warp prior to weaving). Based on ikat, which originated in northeast Asia, *chiné* designs were typically applied to fabrics such as silk taffeta. Often made in muted pastels with floral motifs, *chiné* was favored by Madame de Pompadour, and was often called "Pompadour taffeta." As in life, spies and voyeurs peopled the pages of plays, verses, and novels, as the chaperone in the Paar Room would know all too well. Despite the modesty of her appearance, she is absorbed in *Les Liaisons dangereuses.* The chaperone's reverie evokes that of the figure in Jean-Honoré Fragonard's *Young Woman Reading* (ca. 1780, p. 124), which hangs in the room, paving the way for the music tutor's erotic advances toward her chaste charge.

THE WITHDRAWING ROOM: A HELPFUL VALET
VARENGEVILLE ROOM (PARIS, CA. 1736–52)

Lavish balls at court and in private residences were extremely fashionable throughout the eighteenth century, not least because of the indulgent amusements they encouraged. Eating, drinking, dancing, and conversing promoted an intoxicating atmosphere of flirtatious merrymaking, with men and women appealing to each other's sensory discriminations. Balls, especially royal balls, presented the nobility with a ready opportunity to demonstrate the artfulness of their corporeal governance. Dance, in particular, offered an expressive paradigm for the appraisal of elite bodily presentation. Couples dancing, as represented in *Le Bal paré* (1774, p. 58) by Augustin de Saint-Aubin, was especially au courant in the ancien régime. Not only did it allow individuals to display their own aristocratic comportment but it also allowed them to observe that of others, based, as most couples dancing was, on a series of constantly changing diagonals. The minuet was one of the most popular dances of the period. As Sarah R. Cohen explains in *Art, Dance, and the Body in French Culture of the Ancien Régime* (2000), the minuet began symmetrically with bows and promenading, after which the dancers moved into opposite corners on a diagonal to embark on the minuet's central Z- or S-configuration. Repeated over and over again, this spatial tracery echoed the physical turns and twists of the celebrants, most notably their delicate step patterns and flowing arm gestures, which, in the case of women, were enhanced by lace *engageantes* (small undersleeves with two or three layers of flounces). With its simple structure yet intricate movements, the minuet typified the sensuality of couples dancing, which, through bodily display and interaction, presented an elaborate choreography of seduction.

In the Varengeville Room, which shows a brief interlude from the dizzy social whirl of a grand ball (proving too much for the woman who has fainted and too little for the woman who has caught the eye of an attentive valet), the minuet's swirling gestures and movements are echoed visually in the room's opulent boiserie, which, stylistically, can be assigned to the early phase of the Rococo (just prior to the extreme asymmetry that characterized it between 1736 and 1752). First used in the late eighteenth century, long after the decline of the style's hegemony, the term "Rococo" derived from *rocaille* (after the rocks and shells used to line the walls of grottoes) and came to denote exuberant asymmetrical ornamentation. Like the minuet, the S-line is one of the Rococo's defining features. It organizes the Varengeville's boiseries, the easy, airy carving of which recalls the work of the sculptor and architect Nicolas Pineau, whom the critic Jacques-François Blondel credits with having "invented variety in ornament." The sinuous scrollwork of the paneling includes motifs typical of the style, such as palmettes, bats' wings, foliage sprays, and fantastic birds, but they remain subordinate to its free-flowing, continuous movement.

William Hogarth, a fervent supporter of French Rococo, asserted in his *Analysis of Beauty* (1753) that "the beauty of intricacy lies in contriving winding shapes," which, he maintained, could be applied to all the arts including costume. Stays featured prominently in his discussions, noting that they should not be too straight or too curved. In France during the Rococo period, stays served to raise and form the bosom. Those worn in the Varengeville Room are typically concealed by stomachers, which, in keeping with the splendor of the occasion, are richly adorned with lace, embroidery, and fly fringe (silk floss tied into small knotted tassels). Earlier, in the 1750s, such panels might have revealed a ladder of neatly arranged ribbons, or *échelle*, as seen in François Boucher's portrait of Madame de Pompadour (1759, p. 61). With its ornate three-dimensional decoration, Rococo costume was a Pandora's box of fashion blunders. Few women, however, other than the royal mistress negotiated its excesses and frivolities with such natural panache. As can be seen in the *robes à la française* worn by the women in the room, great ingenuity was used to adorn their surfaces, including padded robings and falbalas, or furbelows. Those applied to some of the gowns, including the one worn by the fainting woman (whose position clearly reveals the shape of her pannier), are made from silver lace, or galloon, which, as can be seen in the armchair, or *fauteuil à la reine*, in the Paar Room, was also used as a trimming for furniture. Several dresses reveal robings with serpentine meanderings, a Rococo flourish that finds visual rapport in the legs and arm supports of the room's Louis XV seat furniture. In a potent display of the collusion between fashion and furniture, the arms of many of the chairs, including the *fauteuil à la reine* made by Nicolas-Quinibert Foliot (covered in its original Beauvais tapestry) have retreated inward to accommodate the period's voluminous ballgowns. S-scrolls also dictate the design of the extraordinary gold-and-scarlet japanned writing table, or *bureau plat*. Made by the royal cabinetmaker Gilles Joubert for Louis XV's study at Versailles, its chinoiserie decoration establishes a sensual relationship with a group of opulent gowns with exoticized design elements relating to the iconography of three of the known continents. One is woven with leopard spots evoking Africa, another is brocaded with Asian-inspired pagodas, and a third is woven with bands of ermine suggesting the bounteous New World (Alaska being one of the ermine's natural habitats). To the far right of this group is a lavish gown brocaded with Roman ruins, an early example of the influence of antiquity, which affected the applied arts in France from the mid-eighteenth century. While the table's gracefully contoured legs recall those of an elegant *femme du monde*, its ormolu sabots evoke her delicate footwear. For much of the eighteenth century, women's petticoats were raised slightly to reveal their shoes, which were exquisitely rendered in silks, damasks, and brocades. Although the colors and materials of women's footwear usually reflected the elegance of their robes, they rarely matched, except for the most formal occasions. From the 1770s the heels of shoes moved toward the instep, producing a light, tiptoeing gait. When worn for dancing, they not only enhanced the grace and agility of a woman's performance but also the coquetry of her corporeal artifice.

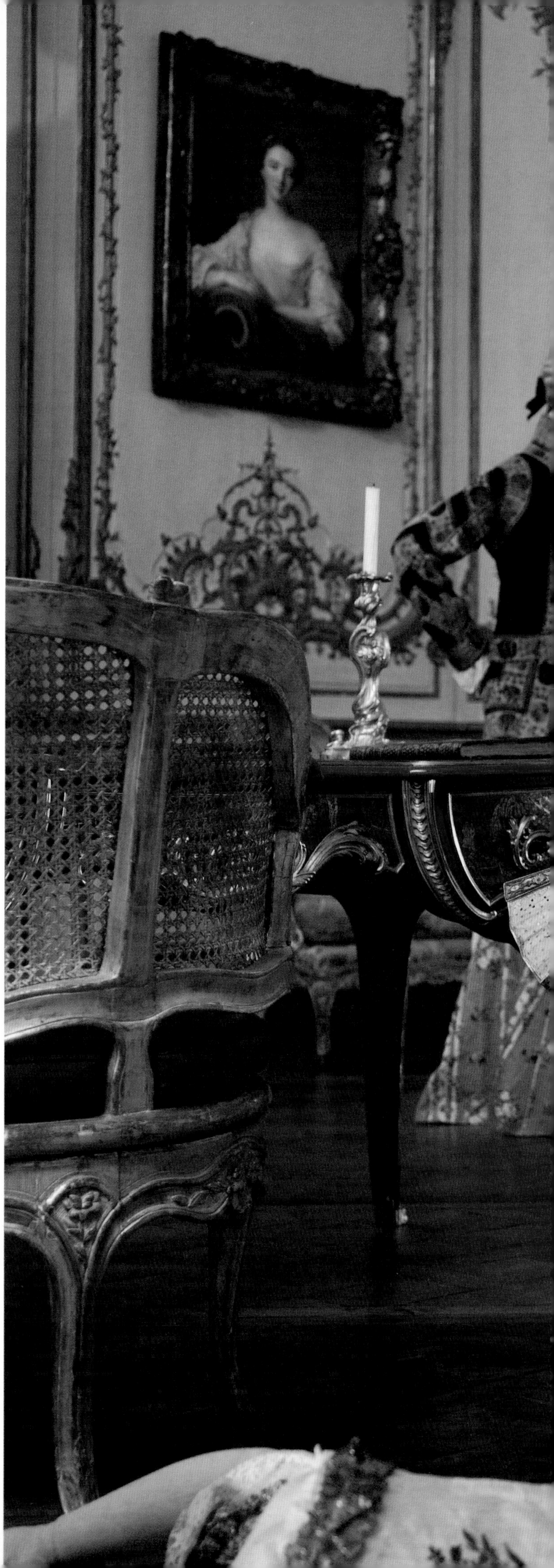

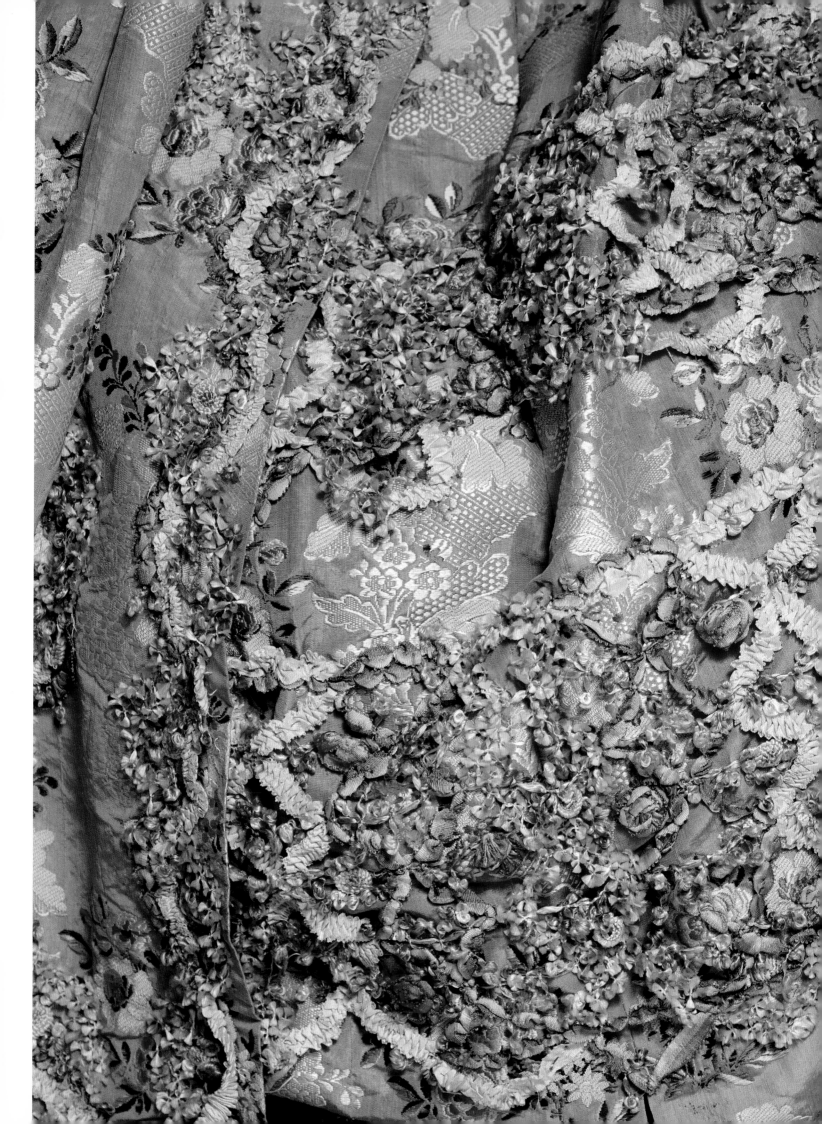

THE MASKED BEAUTY
ROCOCO ROOM (FRENCH, CA. 1730–35)

The custom of masking, which dates back to antiquity, reached its apogee in the eighteenth century. For a society governed by the pursuit of pleasure, the appeal of disguise lay in the liberties it allowed. Negotiating the slippage between reality and fantasy, dress as deception provided endless possibilities for social and sexual adventures through the subversion of age, sex, race, and class identities. Although every level of society practiced masquerading, the nobility realized its greatest potential for role-playing through elite social gatherings such as pageants and fêtes galantes, rural masquerades with narratives immortalized by Nicolas Lancret, Jean-Antoine Watteau, and Jean-Baptiste-Joseph Pater. However, the dynamic versatility of masking was most fully exploited at court balls, occasions for the parade of every imaginable character, real or fictional, exotic or pastoral, heroic or theatrical. Indeed, it was not unusual for guests to change their costumes during the course of an evening, adding to the spiraling confusions of the masquerade. Louis XV appreciated the shifting identities and theatrical performances of masquerading. In 1745, when the dauphin was married to Infanta Maria Theresa of Spain, the king staged a lavish masked ball in the Galerie des Glaces at Versailles. In the watercolor by Charles-Nicolas Cochin II (1745, p. 79), guests arrive in a mélange of costumes and disguises. The dauphin and his new wife appeared as a shepherd and shepherdess, while Louis XV and a group of attendant courtiers came as clipped yew trees from the palace gardens. In the watercolor the king is portrayed talking to a woman dressed as a huntress to his right, while behind him is a shepherdess, both of whom, depending on the source, have been interpreted as Madame d'Étioles, later Madame de Pompadour, who was a guest at the ball. Subsequently, she was to be painted in both guises, as Diana by Jean-Marc Nattier (1748), and as *La Belle Jardinière* by Carle van Loo (ca. 1754–55). The latter portrait evoked her love of nature and gardening, an interest evident in the theatrical pastorals she produced and starred in for the king's amusement at Versailles. Over their usual court dress, many of the guests, as depicted in the watercolor, wore the domino. Consisting of a full, long gown with a hood, it was worn by both men and women when they did not wish to wear fancy dress. Along with a mask, the domino was the most basic form of court (and carnival) disguise. Such gowns, which were usually made of silk, covered the clothes beneath, creating a visual disequilibrium that rendered suspect any positive identification.

A fan is used by the masked beauty to conceal her identity. Painted with a white mask, the fan parodies the trompe l'oeil effects of masquerading. In the eighteenth century fans, like swords for men, were romantic adjuncts to a woman's costume. They served as aids for the elegant display of the hands, as well as for the subtle aspects of courtship, giving rise to a complex sign language that was taught in a special academy in London. Noting such visual communication, the essayist Joseph Addison observed in *The Spectator* (1711): "Women are armed with fans as men with swords, and sometimes do more execution with them. . . . I have seen a fan so very angry that it would have been dangerous for the absent lover who provoked it to have come within the wind of it, and at other times so very languishing that I have been glad for the lady's sake that the lover was at a sufficient distance from it. I need not add that a fan is either a prude or a coquette, according to the nature of the person who bears it." Like fans, ribbons worn in knots at the arms, waist, and bosom were part of the vocabulary of allusion, as were patches worn on the face.

With its intricate hand-painted detailing, the fan abets the aesthetic dynamism of the masked beauty's elaborately embellished *robe à la française*. Made of silk satin with silver floral brocade and bobbin-lace trimming, its padded robings and furbelows promote a visual intensity heightened by the robe's proportions. The eighteenth-century impulse to exaggerate decoratively was satisfied corporeally through stays and the pannier, infra-edifices that, in their ability to conceal a woman's natural contours, extended the paradigm of masquerading. Usually made of whalebone, stays, which arrived in France from Spain in the sixteenth century, served to raise the bust, narrow the waist, and force the shoulders back. Reinforced with a center-front steel strip, or busk, effecting a ramrod posture critical to elite self-display, stays required a woman to bend at the hips rather than at the waist. A popular conceit of the period, often represented in caricatures, was that of a woman removing her busk to fend off the advances of an ardent admirer. By drawing attention to the principal physical and symbolic obstacle to her virtue, however, the busk was less an object of punishment than of provocation. Usually, small hip pads were attached to stays to support the pannier, a hooped petticoat made of cane, metal, wood, or whalebone. A relative of the sixteenth century *vertugade*, or farthingale, the pannier, so-called because of its resemblance to a cage, first appeared in France in 1718. As Madeleine Delpierre notes in *Dress in France in the Eighteenth Century* (1997), its initial form was a small, truncated cone, but from 1725 it gradually developed into a large, bell-shaped dome. By about 1740 the pannier grew more elliptical, the result of a system of internal pulleys, and around the mid-eighteenth century it divided into two cages fastened together with tape or cords. Known as "elbow panniers" or "comfort panniers," because the forearms could be rested on them, they varied in depth and extension. Extreme versions, usually reserved for the most formal occasions, created a narrow, flattened silhouette that demanded acute spatial perspicacity. As shown in *Les Adieux* (1777) by Jean-Michel Moreau le Jeune (p. 76), such a widened hipline required a woman to pass through a doorway sideways. Henry Fielding in his novel *Tom Jones* (1749) describes such a spectacle: "In short, a footman knocked, or rather thundered, at the door. . . . The door of the room flew open, and after pushing in her hoop sideways before her, entered Lady Bellaston."

The Favorite
Rococo Room (French, ca. 1730–35)

Writing about France in the 1770s and 1780s, the artist Élisabeth Vigée-Lebrun declared, with more than a soupçon of self-regard, "Women reigned." This, at least in terms of their social status, was the case for most of the century. Indeed, in an age when wit, charm, and intelligence were the measure of both men and women, the sexes were equally pitched. Of all the social settings in which men and women converged, the salon offered a lively context for women to assert their cultural authority. One of the first to realize its social and intellectual possibilities was Madame du Deffand, who entertained some of the greatest artists, writers, politicians, and philosophers of the Enlightenment. In his edition of her letters the writer Horace Walpole described how the *salonnière* embodied "the graces of the most polished style which, however, are less beautiful than the graces of the wit they clothe." Madame du Deffand, however, was but one of a coterie of women who greatly affected the literary and artistic traditions of the period. Voltaire's lover, the marquise du Châtelet, was a prodigious and disciplined intellectual known for her writings on metaphysics. Blessed with beauty as well as brains, it was said that when she visited Louis XV (opposite, as a child), she placed two rubies over her nipples, much to the king's delight. Louis XV was a serial adulterer. He is alleged, however, to have given his wife, Queen Marie Leszcynska, who bore him ten children, "seven proofs of love" on the night of their wedding. While he took many lovers, few women attained the coveted position of favorite, or official royal mistress. Among the exceptions were Madame de Pompadour and Madame du Barry, who became two of the most powerful women of the Enlightenment.

The two favorites made themselves indispensable to Louis XV, acting as lovers and confidantes, as well as policy advisers and ministerial consultants. Many official royal mistresses, or *maîtresses en titre*, before them had played a role in state business, but Madame de Pompadour and Madame du Barry greatly extended the position to promote their own and the king's policies. This was all the more extraordinary given that neither woman was born into the aristocracy, the usual reserve for royal mistresses. Pompadour's background was middle class, or bourgeois at best, and Barry's working class. However, what they lacked in terms of their social backgrounds, they more than made up for in terms of their beauty. Before Pompadour met Louis XV, the wit and magistrate President Hénault, after meeting her at the Opéra, told Madame du Deffand that Pompadour was "one of the prettiest women I have ever seen," adding that "she understands music perfectly, sings with all the gaiety and good taste imaginable, knows by heart a hundred songs and takes part in plays." On becoming the king's mistress, Pompadour served as the unofficial cultural minister, commissioning and collaborating with some of the most important artists, craftsmen, and practitioners of the Rococo.

Madame de Pompadour's taste in dress reflected the visual arts she promoted. Unlike the pious Queen Marie Leszcynska, who, like her daughters, showed little interest in clothes, Pompadour was the mirror of fashion. She defined the elegance of the Rococo, as seen in the many portraits of her by François Boucher. In what is arguably Boucher's finest, painted in 1756 and shown at the Salon the following year (p. 6), her status as fashion arbiter is plainly evident in a *robe à la française* that seems to take over the picture. Made from emerald green silk taffeta, it is decorated with frilled robings and furbelows with applied pink silk roses. Her stomacher is richly adorned with a ladder of ribbons, or *échelle*, of pink silk taffeta with silver stripes. Matching ribbons are tied around her neck and applied to her flared sleeve cuffs, below which appear lace *engageantes*. With roses in her hair, strings of pearls at her wrists, and pink satin mules on her feet (arched with "Louis" heels that reflect the elegance of the ormolu sabots on the writing table beside her), the overall image is one of elegant harmony. She wears an equally graceful *robe à la française* in Boucher's last portrait, painted in 1759 (p. 61). By now in her late thirties, Pompadour is still portrayed as a young, beautiful woman, a testament to her skills in the arts of image making.

Although Madame du Barry did not exert the same influence on costume as her predecessor, she had a keen interest in fashion. As a girl, she had been employed by one of the most exclusive boutiques in Paris owned by Monsieur Labille (the father of Adélaïde Labille-Guiard). Joan Haslip argues in *Madame du Barry* (2005) that it was while working for Labille that Barry learned to dress in the pale colors that best suited her blue eyes and blonde hair. Madame du Barry's beauty was even more legendary than Pompadour's. Recalling his first meeting with her, Monsieur Belleval wrote in his memoirs: "I can still see her carelessly seated or rather reclining in a large easy chair, wearing a white dress with wreaths of roses. She was one of the prettiest women at a court which boasted so many, and the very perfection of her loveliness made her the most fascinating." Madame du Barry affected a romantic carelessness in her appearance, and, like her rival Marie-Antoinette, favored the simple cotton chemise not only for the comfort it afforded but also because it revealed her famous bosom to great effect. In contrast to Marie-Antoinette's more modest appearance in her portrait attributed to Vigée-Lebrun (p. 8), Barry dared to pose for the artist François-Hubert Drouais in a sheer cotton chemise with a hint of her right nipple showing (p. 85). She would often dine with the king in such attire, her hair loosely knotted and decorated with flowers. Despite her fondness for dressing *en déshabillé*, etiquette demanded that she wear the *robe à la française* for formal occasions. From the 1770s the style became less popular as everyday fashion, but it was still worn at court, maintaining tradition as well as its namesake. As can be seen by the version worn by "The Favorite" arranging flowers, a reference to another painting of Barry by Drouais, formal dress was still meant to dazzle through the opulence of its materials and the exaggeration of its silhouette.

THE BROKEN VASE: A CONSOLING MERCHANT
SÈVRES ROOM (FRENCH, CA. 1770)

Luxury objects were pivotal to the formation of aristocratic identity in the ancien régime, serving as powerful statements of affluence and, more importantly, aesthetic discrimination. Elite men and women, recognizing their symbolic significance, consumed decorative artworks with an appetite that was as audacious as it was rapacious. Madame de Pompadour, in particular, was known for her voracious consumption of extravagant commodities. In *Madame de Pompadour* (2002), Colin Jones notes that after her death in 1764 it took a team of specialists more than two years to prepare for the auction of her prodigious collection (which, during her lifetime, was dispersed among her numerous properties, including Crécy, Bellevue, and the Hôtel d'Évreux, and, to a large extent, reserved for the private delectation of the king and their circle of friends). Twenty years after the sale, the writer Louis-Sébastien Mercier recalled "the admiration mixed with amazement" elicited by viewing Pompadour's wealth of "objects of luxury, fantasy and magnificence." Although her obsession for decoration extended across the spectrum of the applied arts, her greatest passion was porcelain. In an attempt to serve the state and enhance royal popularity, she directed her attention to French-produced porcelain. To support local manufactories, which reduced France's dependence on imports and attracted foreign currency to the country, was, in Pompadour's words "to be a good citizen." It was a role she took seriously (and one that extended to the Paris garment industry, which enlisted her as a mannequin). She was instrumental in establishing the Manufacture royale de Sèvres (1759), with which her name became associated. Most of the porcelain she purchased was in a variety of blues and whites (the "rose Pompadour" seems to have gained its name after her death). Louis XV shared his favorite's interest in porcelain and bought for himself 25,000 *livres* of Sèvres each year. In the cause of national interest, a shop was opened on the rue de la Monnaie (just off the rue Saint-Honoré, which, by the mid-eighteenth century, had become a major center of the trade in luxury goods) as a *dépôt royal des porcelains de Sèvres*.

Shopping was an important component of eighteenth-century aristocratic experience. Indeed, the shops where luxury objects were sold were places for sociability as well as seduction, themes explored in "The Shop" (p. 116) and "The Broken Vase," the latter based on a conflation of Jean-Antoine Watteau's *Gersaint's Shop Sign* (1720, p. 88), and Michel Garnier's The *Poorly Defended Rose* (1789, p. 91). While Watteau's painting provides the context for the Sèvres Room's vignette, Garnier's provides the denouement, notably a merchant, or *marchand mercier,* embracing a young woman whose elderly husband is inspecting a jewel coffer, or *coffre à bijoux,* mounted with Sèvres porcelain plaques. As in Garnier's painting, the vignette is infused with symbols of love, such as the closed jewel coffer and the hand-painted flowers on the Sèvres plaques, which are mirrored on the young woman's *robe à la polonaise*. Referencing the origins of porcelain, the robe is made from Chinese silk, the color of which reflects the so-called biscuit developed by Sèvres. The scene, like Garnier's painting, is also infused with symbols of loss of virtue, such as the broken vase and the two dogs that have leapt from the arms of their mistress. In eighteenth-century portraiture dogs frequently appeared as symbols of devotion. Madame de Pompadour, revealing her loyalty to Louis XV, was often painted with her two beloved papillons, Inès and Mimi, who were known also as "Fidelity" and "Constancy," respectively. Pompadour was so attached to her dogs that she commissioned several portraits of them, including one that appeared on the lid of a Sèvres porcelain snuffbox. In François Boucher's last portrait of her (p. 61), in which she is in a garden setting dressed in a typical Rococo confection, Inès is sitting on a bench, her devotion to her mistress mirroring her mistress's devotion to her king.

It is likely that the jewel coffer attributed to Martin Carlin was commissioned by Pompadour's successor, Madame du Barry. Sèvres-mounted porcelain furniture appealed primarily to female clients, many of whom, like Madame du Barry, patronized the *marchands merciers* Simon-Philippe Poirier and his partner and successor Dominique Daguerre, principal purchasers of porcelain plaques from the Sèvres manufactory. While the guild regulations of *marchands merciers* forbade them to make luxury objects, they were permitted to commission pieces and to facilitate production by supplying design and even materials to artisans and manufactories. The same rules applied to *marchands de modes,* the ancestors of the *grand couturiers* of the nineteenth century. Suppliers of trimmings and accessories, *marchands de modes* practiced a way of working that was creative and conceptual rather than manual and mechanical. Perhaps the most celebrated *marchand de mode* of the eighteenth century was Rose Bertin, who came to public attention when, while working for the *maîtresse couturière* Mademoiselle Pagelle, she made the wedding trousseau of the duchesse de Chartres. Although the work of the *maîtresse couturière,* who made the garments, and that of the *marchand de mode,* who trimmed them, were separate in the guild system of the ancien régime, the fact that Bertin achieved such eminence illustrates the importance attached to trimmings, or *agreements,* by fashionable women. After she opened her own business in 1770, Bertin used her fertile imagination, her talent as a businesswoman, and her knack for self-publicity to dictate the rules of fashion to all the courts of Europe. Her most famous client, however, was Marie-Antoinette. Bertin's biweekly meetings with the queen earned her the soubriquet "Minister of Fashion." She continued to supply Marie-Antoinette with trimmings and accessories after the queen's arrest and imprisonment in the Temple during the French Revolution (1789–99). Marie-Antoinette's extravagance in matters of dress was notorious. Indeed, the queen's profligacy weighed heavily against her during her trial, which, ultimately, ended in her death on October 16, 1793, at the blade of "Saint Guillotine."

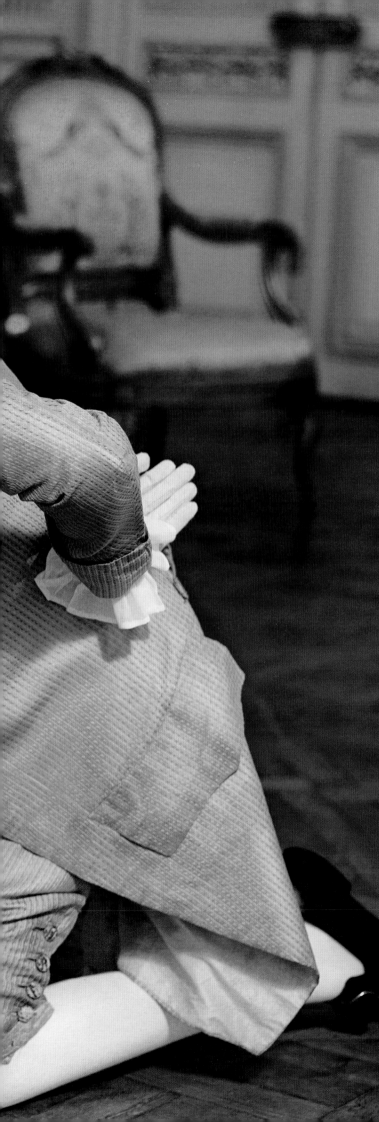

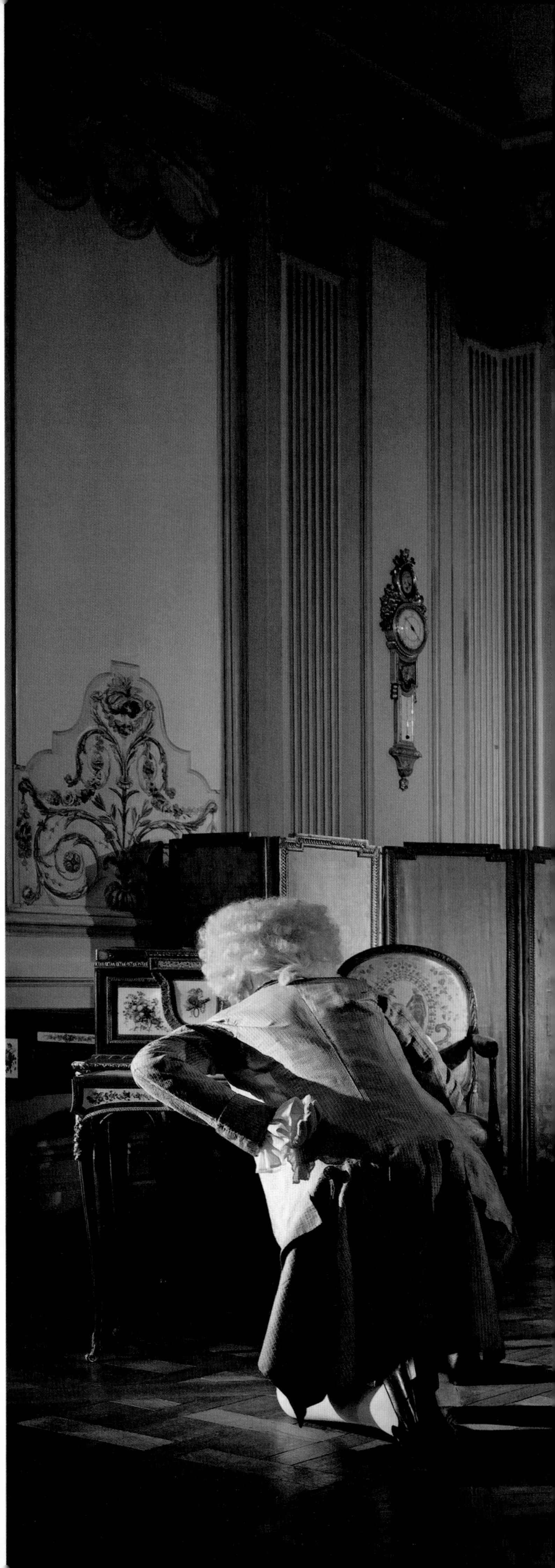

THE CARD GAME: CHEATING AT *CAVAGNOLE*
BORDEAUX ROOM (BORDEAUX, CA. 1785)

In Jean-François de Bastide's erotic architectural novella *La Petite Maison* (1758), a round salon "unequalled in all the universe" served as the initial (interior) setting for the sensory education of the virtuous Mélite by the cultivated Marquis de Tremicour. "So voluptuous was this salon," wrote Bastide, "that it inspired the tenderest feelings, feelings that one believes one could have only for its owner." Small, curved rooms became particularly fashionable during the late eighteenth century. Used as cabinets, boudoirs, or bedchambers in the private apartments of hôtels and mansions, their size, shape, and status encouraged intimacy and informality. Negating the presence of servants, many ovoid or round rooms were fitted with mechanical conveyances such as dumbwaiters and *tables volantes,* or *tables machinées.* Used as an instrument of seduction in *La Petite Maison,* a multitask version of a *table volante* is described in the *Mercure de France*: "When the guests enter the room, not a single trace of the table would be visible; they see only a very open parquet with an ornamental rose at the center. At the slightest signal, the petals withdraw under the parquet and the served table springs up, accompanied by four dumbwaiters which rise through four openings at the same time." Such feats of technical trickery actively enhanced an ovoid or round room's potential for dalliance.

The Bordeaux Room, which was originally serviced by a dumbwaiter, reveals its mischievous possibilities through a game of chance. During the ancien régime gambling was ubiquitous, as evidenced in paintings and engravings from the period, such as Pierre Louis Dumesnil le Jeune's *Interior with Card Players* (ca. 1750–60, p. 98), and Jean-Michel Moreau le Jeune's *La Partie de whist* (1788, p. 101). As Thomas M. Kavanagh observes in *Enlightenment and the Shadows of Chance* (1993), this epidemic was in no small part due to the example set by the nobility, who gambled with dizzying intensity and alarming regularity. Central to the social rituals of the aristocracy, gambling, or rather the revenue generated from gambling, helped to offset the lavish receptions hosted by the nobility. Most lucrative were *jeux de hasard* such as *hoca, biribi,* basset, *pharaon,* and lansquenet, as opposed to *jeux de commerce*, in which skill played more of a role than the chance-driven turning of a card, rolling of a die, or picking of a number. In the Bordeaux Room two men and two women are indulging in a *jeu de hasard* known as *cavagnole*, an early form of lotto. One of the women, abetted by an abbé in his role as cicisbeo, is cheating. If the abbé's status, announced by his black "suit of office" (an outward symbol of his piety and righteousness) works to the woman's advantage, so does the chair on which he is seated. Known as a viewer, or *voyeuse*, it was designed specifically for gaming sessions and was produced in a variety of different models depending on the sitter's gender. With its high, saddle-shaped seat, the chair in the Bordeaux Room, which is attributed to Sulpice Brizard, was designed for a male spectator. Straddling it backward, he could rest his arms on the top rail of the chair and watch the game unfold. While a *voyeuse*, through its design and function, allowed a spectator to view the hand of a player (and in the case of the abbé literally support his duplicity), a game table, such as the one in the room attributed to Bernard II van Risenburgh, prevented such a privilege between participants. Although the size of the table, or *table à jouer*, brought players into close proximity, the legs as well as the rounded corners of the playing surface (designed to support candlesticks) limited and controlled this proximity, protecting each player's hand and preventing the possibility of cheating.

As a social practice among the aristocracy, gambling on such high-stake games as *cavagnole* was governed by a strict code of ethics. A true nobleman never gambled purely for the purpose of winning, but to show his indifference to and independence from money as a commodity. Cheating revealed a person's social inferiority by indicating an immoderate attachment to financial attainment. To gamble for gain was to equate social status with wealth, an ethos that was regarded as distinctly bourgeois. Gambling avariciously involved the application of reason and probability, an approach that was seemingly antithetical to the aristocracy. Ironically, the ideal of rationality became the grounds upon which bourgeois moralists condemned gambling during the eighteenth century. This ideology reflected the intellectual posturings of French Enlightenment philosophers such as Voltaire and Denis Diderot, who advocated rationality as a means to establish a system of ethics, aesthetics, and knowledge. In art their teachings came to be associated with Neoclassicism, a style, which, impelled by excavations at Herculaneum in 1738, gradually replaced the Rococo from the mid-eighteenth century. Defined by its rigor and sobriety, the style suffuses the decoration of the Bordeaux Room. The rational austerity of the room's boiserie, attributed to Barthélemy Cabirol and his workshop, are typical of Neoclassicism's restraining and regularizing tendencies. This same impulse to control and organize can be seen in the clarified carvings of the Bordeaux Room's furniture, particularly in the chairs on which the players are seated. Typical of the aesthetic coherence of eighteenth-century French decorative arts, their strict lines extend to the textiles of the men's *habits à la française* and the women's *robes à la française*, the simple stripes of which represent a distillation of the aesthetic principles of Neoclassicism. Striped fabrics began to make their appearance in the 1760s, although it was not until the mid-1770s that they came to replace the curving ribbons and sinuous garlands of flowers that had been so much an aspect of Rococo fashions. While the cotton chemise worn by Madame du Barry and Marie-Antoinette revealed a nascent classicism, it was not until the mid-1790s (when women finally abandoned their stays and panniers) that the *goût grec* fully impacted on fashion in the form of the Directoire style.

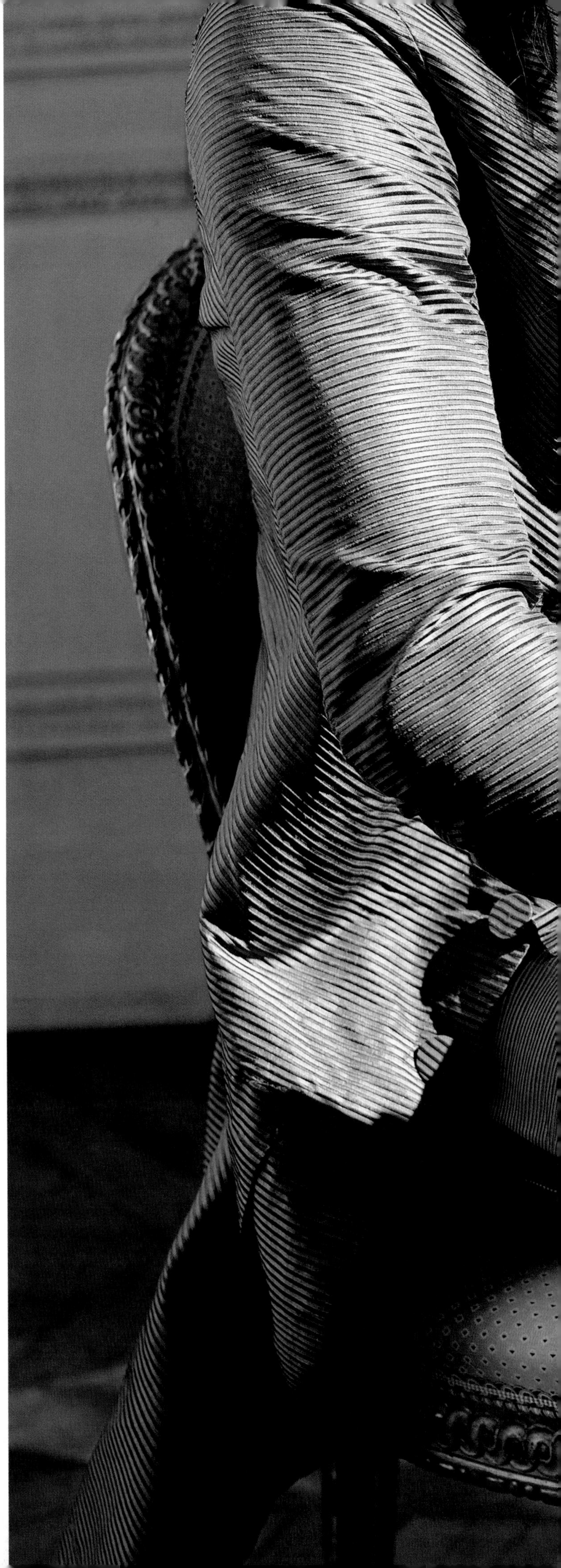

THE LATE SUPPER: THE MEMENTO
CRILLON ROOM (PARIS, CA. 1777–80)

In the eighteenth century the notion of chance, or *le hazard*, was not limited to high-stakes gambling, but actually sustained and regulated elite social interactions, particularly those of the libertine and the voluptuary. Chance as a strategy of seduction provided a thematics of representation for artists like François Boucher, Jean-Antoine Watteau, and Jean-Honoré Fragonard, and for writers such as Denis Diderot, Crébillon fils, and Choderlos de Laclos. As Catherine Cusset explains in *The Libertine Reader* (1997), pleasure as the product of chance propels the narrative of Dominique Vivant Denon's *Point de lendemain* (1777), a short novella of a one-night affair without sequel and, seemingly, without consequences. One evening, as the young narrator (who is not named) waits for his mistress to join him at the Opéra, he is abducted by the beautiful and manipulative Mme de T—— and is taken to a château outside Paris, where they make love deliciously and repeatedly. Whenever an erotic contact occurs between the two protagonists, it is ascribed to chance, as is their first physical encounter: "The lurching of the carriage [on the journey toward the château] caused Mme de T——'s face to touch mine. At an unexpected jolt, she grasped my hand; and I, by the purest chance, caught hold of her in my arms." Chance enables Mme de T—— to preserve "certain principles of decency to which she was scrupulously attached," while, at the same time, it allows her to advance and acquiesce to the narrator's lovemaking. In the final scene of seduction, which occurs in a secret chamber covered in mirrors, these "principles of decency" are revealed for what they are, pretenses of decency. At the same time this "vast cage of mirrors" exposes chance for what it is, a veil and a vehicle for physical pleasure.

Mirrors reflect and inflame the libidinous enterprise in the Crillon Room, a polyhedral *cabinet des glaces* decorated about the same time that Denon published *Point de lendemain*. While many materials were used for inserts to boiserie in the eighteenth century, such as velvets, brocades, and tapestries, mirrors held a unique position because of their ability to augment a room's spatial, ornamental, and luminescent arrangement. Enchanted by their reflective amplification, Horace Walpole, in a letter to

George Selwyn on September 16, 1776, writes: "Madame de Marchais . . . has a house in a nut-shell, that is fuller of inventions than a fairy-tale; her bed stands in the middle of the room because there is no other space that would hold it; and is surrounded by such a perspective of looking glasses, that you may see all that passes in it from the first antechamber." Mirror rooms, which appeared in French domestic architecture from the end of the sixteenth century, were costly marks of distinction. Even after the invention of plate glass in the late seventeenth century, a technique that increased the speed of production as well as the size and weight of the mirrors themselves, the larger versions required for a *cabinet des glaces* remained beyond the reach of all but a few.

The taste for reflection in the eighteenth century was disseminated through fashionable engravings, such as Jean-Michel Moreau le Jeune's *N'Ayez pas peur ma bonne amie* (1776, p. 126). It shows a young woman lying on a sofa in a niche, the back wall of which is mirrored in a similar manner to the recess in the Crillon Room. Like the illustration, the Crillon's mirrored crevice promotes a sense of intimacy and playfulness. The mise-en-scène shows a woman in an exquisite *robe à la française* with her *compères* unhooked to reveal her corset. *Compères*, which were introduced as an alternative to the stomacher in the mid- to late-1760s, were two flaps of fabric that formed a false waistcoat fastened with hooks or buttons. In her hand is one of her garters, which she is about to give to her suitor as a memento of their erotic encounter. Garters, which usually consisted of a silk ribbon tied just above the knee to hold up the stockings, were often embroidered with sexual sayings. Madeleine Delpierre notes (1997) that from the 1770s garters became more elaborate and could even take the form of a small satin bracelet in two halves, one bearing springs inside to act as elastic, the other decorated with amorous devices. The Cabris Room's vignette is a conflation of Jean-François de Troy's *The Garter* (p. 108) and *The Declaration of Love* (p. 111), painted in 1724. Conceived as pendants, these *tableaux de mode* present two scenes of seduction acted out in opulent interiors that serve as a catalogue of French interior design of the period. Both reveal wall surfaces that have been painted, a treatment popular in the early eighteenth century and one revived through the influences of Neoclassicism, as seen in the delicately painted boiserie in the Crillon Room. Designed by Pierre-Adrien Pâris and executed by an unknown artist, the panels are based on a series of arabesques painted by Raphael and his assistants on the walls of the Vatican loggias in the early sixteenth century. Imbued with a Neoclassical sensibility, the Crillon Room's boiseries act as a sumptuous backdrop for the woman's ravishing *robe à la française*, made from silk taffeta painted with stripes and flowers in the easy style of the wall panels, and also for the resplendent Neoclassical furniture. The daybed and the armchair, resting on legs inspired by Ionic columns, were made in 1788 by Jean-Baptiste-Claude Sené for Marie-Antoinette's *cabinet de toilette* at the Château de Saint-Cloud. The two uprights on the front of the daybed, as well as the armrest supports of the chair, are carved with busts of Egyptian maidens. Egyptianizing iconography was introduced in the 1770s and became fairly widespread in the 1780s. At the turn of the nineteenth century Vivant Denon exposed the allure of Egypt to a wider European audience through the publication of his *Voyage dans la basse et haute Egypte* (1803). An account of his expedition with Napoleon in 1798, this travelogue revealed the diversity and richness of Egyptian antiquities just as astutely as his *Point de lendemain* had disclosed the licentious stratagems of the libertine and the voluptuary.

FRONTISPIECE

THE PORTRAIT: AN UNEXPECTED
ENTANGLEMENT

Suit (*Habit à la française*). French, 1780–89. Black silk
pile voided velvet with dark red faille ground and
multicolored floral silk embroidery, ivory silk satin
with multicolored floral silk embroidery. Rogers
Fund, 1932 (32.40a–c)

**Formal Reception Room from the Hôtel de Tessé,
Paris (ca. 1768–72)**
The Hôtel de Tessé, at 1 quai Voltaire, Paris, was built
for Marie-Charlotte de Béthune-Charost, widow of
Comte René de Tessé, between 1765 and 1768. The
plans are attributed to Pierre-Noël Rousset (1715–
1793), a member of the Académie Royale d'Architecture. The interior decoration was probably complet-
ed by the time the final payment was made, on April 9,
1772, to the architect and contractor Louis Letellier
(died 1785). The windows of this room opened on to a
balcony overlooking the Seine and the Louvre beyond.
The room, referred to as the *salle du dais*, or canopy
room, in the inventory drawn up after the death of the
comtesse de Tessé in 1783, was used for official receptions and for ceremonial transactions, during which the
comtesse sat under a crimson damask canopy embroidered with gold thread.

The Painter
Dress (*Robe retroussée dans les poches*). French, 1770–90.
Rose, pale green, and dark brown tartan silk taffeta.
Purchase, Irene Lewisohn Bequest, 1964 (C.I.64.33a, b)

The Sitter
Dress (*Robe à l'anglaise*). French, 1784–87. White cotton
muslin with hammered silver thread embroidery. Isabel
Shults Fund, 1991 (1991.204a, b)

Daybed (*Duchesse en bateau*). French, ca. 1770. Jean-
Baptiste II Lelarge (1711–1771). Carved and gilded
beech, modern cinnamon-colored silk velvet. Purchase,
Mrs. Charles Wrightsman Gift, 1987 (1987.188a, b)

The Sitter's Husband
Dressing Gown. French, second half of the eighteenth
century. Rose and light gray faille with multicolored silk
floral brocade. Purchase, Estate of Irene Lewisohn and
Alice Crowley, 1976 (1976.149.1)

Mechanical Table (*Table mécanique*). French, 1778. Jean-
Henri Riesener (1734–1806). Oak veneered with *bois
satiné*, holly, amaranth, barberry, sycamore, and green
lacquered wood, gilt bronze. Rogers Fund, 1933 (33.12)

The Sitter's Friend
Dress (*Robe à l'anglaise*). French, 1785–87. Ivory and
pink striped silk taffeta. Purchase, Irene Lewisohn
Bequest, 1966 (C.I.66.39a, b)

Paneling (*Boiserie*). French, 1768–72, with later additions. Carved, painted, and gilded oak. Gift of Mrs.
Herbert N. Straus, 1942 (42.203.1)

THE LEVÉE: THE ASSIDUOUS ADMIRER

THE MUSIC LESSON: A WINDOW OF
OPPORTUNITY

Room from the Hôtel de Cabris, Grasse (ca. 1775–78)

The Hôtel de Cabris, in the town of Grasse, in southern France, is now a local museum. It was built between 1771 and 1774 for Jean-Paul de Clapiers, marquis de Cabris, and his wife, née Louise de Mirabeau, who hired the little-known Milanese architect Giovanni Orello. The oak paneling, which was carved, painted, and gilded in Paris, is described in a 1778 inventory of the hôtel as still being packed in crates. Owing to the vicissitudes suffered by the Cabris family (the marquis was declared insane in 1777) and the upheavals of the French Revolution, this paneling may not have been unpacked or installed until the early nineteenth century. It was then assembled in the space originally intended for a small reception room, or *salon de compagnie*, behind the first two windows to the left of the central projecting block on the second floor. Photographs taken of the room when it was in situ show that there were originally five mirrors and five pairs of double doors. The fifth pair was located in the center of the wall opposite the windows and was flanked by mirrors. The Carrara marble chimneypiece, contemporary with but not original to the room, was formerly in the Hôtel de Greffuhle, 8–10 rue d'Astorg, Paris.

The Woman

Peignoir. French, mid- to late eighteenth century. White linen with blue ribbon trim. Courtesy of Lillian Williams

Stays. European, third quarter of the eighteenth century. Pale blue linen with white linen tape trim. Gift of the Jacqueline Loewe Fowler Costume Collection, 1983 (1983.213.4)

Hairdressing Chair (*Fauteuil à coiffer*). French, ca. 1760. Attributed to Louis Delanois (1731–1792). Carved beech. Courtesy of Anthony Victoria

Traveling, Dressing, Writing, and Eating Table (*Table de voyage*). French, 1775–80. Martin Carlin (ca. 1730–1785). Oak and pine veneered with tulipwood, sycamore, holly, boxwood, and ebony, gilt bronze. Gift of Mr. and Mrs. Charles Wrightsman, 1976 (1976.155.99)

Dress (*Robe à la polonaise*). French, 1778–80. Pink silk jacquard with pale green and ivory silk, silk *passementerie* trim. Purchase, Irene Lewisohn Bequest, 1960 (C.I.60.40.3a)

Side Chair (*Chaise à la reine*). French, 1784. Georges Jacob (1739–1814). Carved and gilded walnut, modern pink silk *moiré* damask. Gift of Mr. and Mrs. Charles Wrightsman, 1977 (1977.102.13)

The Admirer

Suit (*Habit à la française*). European, ca. 1770. Pale pink silk faille with multicolored floral embroidery. Purchase, Irene Lewisohn Bequest, 1966 (C.I.66.37.1a–c)

Side Chair (*Chaise à la reine*). French, 1784. Georges Jacob (1739–1814). Carved and gilded walnut, modern pink silk *moiré* damask. Gift of Mr. and Mrs. Charles Wrightsman, 1977 (1977.102.14)

The Hairdresser

Suit (*Habit à la française*). European, ca. 1780. Pale pink silk *moiré* with multicolored floral embroidery. Purchase, Irene Lewisohn Bequest, 1960 (C.I.60.5a–c)

Joseph Legros de Rumigny (French). *L'Art de la coëffure des dames françoises, avec des estampes, ou sont représentées les têtes coeffées*, 1767–70. Hand-colored engravings. Purchase, Friends of The Costume Institute Fund, 2004 (2004.126a–e)

Michael Schmidt (German). *Extra Vermaklyk Lotery-Spel*, ca. 1780. Hand-colored engraved playing cards. Gift of Richard Martin, 1998

Paneling (*Boiserie*). French, 1775–78, with later additions. Carved, painted, and gilded oak. Purchase, Mr. and Mrs. Charles Wrightsman Gift, 1972 (1972.276.1, 2)

Room from the Palais Paar, Vienna (ca. 1765–71)

The paneling of this room comes from the Palais Paar, which stood at Wollzeile 30, in Vienna, until 1938. The large quadrilateral Baroque palace, with a central courtyard, was built about 1630 for the postmaster of the Holy Roman Empire, Baron Johann Christoph von Paar. The stables necessary to conduct the extensive business of a post office were located at the back of the building at street level. Behind the twelve large windows above the two entrances in the main façade were four large state rooms. These rooms and the living quarters on the same floor were completely remodeled between 1765 and 1771 for Count Wenzel Joseph Johann von Paar. According to bills formerly in the possession of the Paar family, architect Isidor Canevale (1730–1786) and sculptor Johann Georg Leithne (1725–1785) carried out this remodeling. The Museum's room is composed of elements from two rooms in the living quarters. Almost all the paneling is original. Only the arched window surrounds on the south wall and the four pairs of frames for the French windows are modern additions. The *brèche d'Alep* marble chimneypiece is of the period but not original to the Palais Paar. The flooring of oak squares, called *parquet de Versailles*, is antique, but the plaster cornice and ceiling are modern.

The Student

Dress (*Robe à la française*). French, ca. 1770. Ivory silk damask. Purchase, Funds from Various Donors, 1999 (1999.41a, b)

Armchair (*Fauteuil à la reine*). French, ca. 1730. Carved and gilded beech, modern blue silk velvet. Gift of Mr. and Mrs. Charles Wrightsman, 1971 (1971.206.11)

Pedal Harp. French, second half of the eighteenth century. Renault et Chatelain (founded 1772). Wood, various materials. Gift of J. Pierpont Morgan, 1907 (07.225.68)

The Music Tutor

Suit (*Habit à la française*). Italian, late eighteenth century. Rose and blue silk *changeant* taffeta with red foil and hammered silver buttons and embroidery. Rogers Fund, 1925 (26.56.16a–c)

THE WITHDRAWING ROOM: A HELPFUL
VALET

Adjustable Music, Reading, and Writing Stand (*Pupitre à crémaillère, servant de table*). French, 1760–65. Attributed to Martin Carlin (ca. 1730–1785). Tulipwood, gilt bronze, brass, steel. Purchase, Gift of Mr. and Mrs. Charles Wrightsman, by exchange, 1983 (1983.433a–c)

Armchair (*Fauteuil à la reine*). French, ca. 1749. Nicolas-Quinibert Foliot (active 1729–76). Carved and gilded oak, original velvet and gold braid. Gift of J. Pierpont Morgan, 1906 (07.225.57)

The Chaperone
Dress (*Robe à la française*). French, third quarter of the eighteenth century. Green and ivory serpentine silk damask with matching fly-fringe trim. Gift of Mrs. Robert Woods Bliss, 1943 (C.I.43.90.49a, b)

The Voyeur
Dress (*Robe à la française*). French, ca. 1765–75. Chiné-patterned silk taffeta. Gift of Fédération de la Soirie, 1950 (50.168.1a, b)

Paneling (*Boiserie*). Austrian, 1769–71, with later additions. Carved, painted, and gilded pine. Purchase, Mr. and Mrs. Charles Wrightsman Gift, 1963 (63.229.1)

Room from the Hôtel de Varengeville, Paris (ca. 1736–52)
The Hôtel de Varengeville, at 217 boulevard Saint-Germain, which is now the Maison de l'Amérique Latine, was built in 1704 by the architect Jacques Gabriel (1667–1742) for the widowed comtesse de Varengeville. In 1732 it was inherited by her daughter, who was married to the great military commander Hector-Louis, duc de Villars. In 1736 Mme de Villars sold the house to Marie-Marguerite d'Allègre, comtesse de Ruppelmonde, who owned it until her death in 1752. The comtesse de Ruppelmonde probably commissioned the paneling. The original room had a semicircular end wall pierced by two windows. The six carved mirror frames, the panels of the chimneypiece wall, and most of the elements of the other three walls are part of the original *boiserie*. The plaster ceiling and cornice are modern, as are the two doorframes (the doors are original) and the carved overdoors fitted with paintings of Autumn and of Poetry by François Boucher (1703–1770), which are signed and dated 1753. Contemporary with but not original to the room are the *fleur-de-pêche* marble chimneypiece and the *parquet de Versailles* floor.

The Fainter
Dress (*Robe à la française*). British, 1765–70. Ivory silk faille with satin self-stripe and multicolored silk, silver *filé*, and hammered silver embroidery with hammered silver bobbin-lace trim. Purchase, Irene Lewisohn Bequest, 1962 (C.I.62.29.1a, b)

Friend 1
Dress (*Robe à la française*). French, 1775–89. White, pink, and pale blue silk *cannelé* with multicolored floral silk brocade and *passementerie* trim. Purchase, Irene Lewisohn Bequest, 1961 (C.I.61.13.1a, b)

Friend 2
Dress (*Robe à la française*). British, ca. 1775. White striped silk *cannelé* with metallic lace trim, white cotton Brussels lace, white silk gauze with white chenille and fly-fringe trim. Courtesy of the Kyoto Costume Institute

Writing Table (*Bureau plat*). French, 1759. Gilles Joubert (1689–1775). Lacquered oak, gilt bronze, modern leather top. Gift of Mr. and Mrs. Charles Wrightsman, 1973 (1973.315.1)

Asia
Dress (*Robe à la française*). French, mid-eighteenth century. Blue and white striped cloth-of-silver with gold tinsel and multicolored floral silk brocade, hammered silver bobbin lace and applied silk rosette trim. Gift of Fédération de la Soirie, 1950 (50.168.2a, b)

Africa
Dress (*Robe à la française*). French, mid-eighteenth century. Pink silk and pulled thread broken serpentine motif with floral silk brocade, *passementerie* trim, and silver braid couched by applied gold bobbin-lace. Fletcher Fund, 1938 (C.I.61.34a, b)

America
Dress (*Robe à la française*). French, ca. 1770. Rosy beige silk faille with polychrome woven floral bouquets on ivory ground with brocades of floral sprays, brown and yellow silk spots, and blue silk berries, *passementerie* trim. Purchase, Irene Lewisohn Bequest, 1961 (38.30.1a, b)

Europe
Dress (*Robe à la française*). French, mid-eighteenth century. Beige silk faille with ivory serpentine floral motif and floral spray silk and gold thread brocade, with weft-directed serpentine gold lace appliqué. Gift of Mrs. Hervey Parke Clark, 1961 (C.I.61.16a, b)

Seated Woman
Dress (*Robe à la française*). French, third quarter of the eighteenth century. Pink faille with ivory lace motif and multicolored floral spray silk brocade, ivory silk ruched ribbon and *passementerie* trim, applied silver bobbin lace. Purchase, Irene Lewisohn Bequest, 1959 (C.I.59.29.1a, b)

THE MASKED BEAUTY

THE FAVORITE

Armchair (*Bergère*). French, ca. 1765. L. Cresson. Carved and gilded beech, modern blue green and beige silk lampas. Gift of Mr. and Mrs. Charles Wrightsman, 1971 (1971.206.6)

Friend
Dress (*Robe à la française*). French, ca. 1775. Pink ribbed silk with white linear silk vine motif and multicolored silk floral brocade with multicolored *passementerie* and scalloped fly-fringe trim. Purchase, Isabel Shults Fund, 2005 (2005.61a, b)

Armchair (*Fauteuil à la reine*). French, 1753. Nicolas-Quinibert Foliot (active 1729–76). Carved and gilded beech, original Beauvais tapestry woven with bird and animal subjects after Jean-Baptiste Oudry (1686–1755). Gift of John D. Rockefeller Jr., 1935 (35.145.9). Purchase, Martha Baird Rockefeller Gift, 1966 (66.60.1)

The Valet
Suit. French, mid- to late eighteenth century. Blue and cream wool, multicolored "coat of arms" trimmings. Courtesy of Lillian Williams

Paneling (*Boiserie*). French, ca. 1735, with later additions. Carved, painted, and gilded oak. Purchase, Mr. and Mrs. Charles Wrightsman Gift, 1963 (63.228.1)

Rococo Room, French (ca. 1730–35)
The oak paneling is part of a larger room from an unidentified setting. The trophies of the seasons, carved on the rounded corner panels, are related to drawings by the designer-sculptor François-Antoine Vassé (1681–1736).

Dress (*Robe à la française*). French or Austrian, ca. 1765. Pale blue silk satin with hammered silver floral brocade and silver bobbin-lace trim. Purchase, Irene Lewisohn Bequest, 2001 (2001.472a, b)

Mask Fan. Spanish, mid- to late eighteenth century. Pale blue and pink painted paper with ivory. Gift of Miss Agnes Miles Carpenter, 1955 (C.I.55.43.17)

Paneling (*Boiserie*). French, ca. 1730–35, with later additions. Carved, painted, and gilded oak. Gift of J. Pierpont Morgan, 1966 (07.225.147)

Rococo Room, French (ca. 1730–35)
The oak paneling is part of a larger room from an unidentified setting. The trophies of the seasons, carved on the rounded corner panels, are related to drawings by the designer-sculptor François-Antoine Vassé (1681–1736).

Dress (*Robe à la française*). French, 1775–79. Ivory striped silk with multicolored floral silk brocade and chenille trim. Courtesy of the Kyoto Costume Institute

Paneling (*Boiserie*). French, ca. 1730–35, with later additions. Carved, painted, and gilded oak. Gift of J. Pierpont Morgan, 1966 (07.225.147)

THE BROKEN VASE: A CONSOLING
MERCHANT

THE CARD GAME: CHEATING AT
CAVAGNOLE

The Sèvres Room, French (ca. 1770)

The oak paneling in this room was acquired by Baron
Frédéric-Jérôme Pichon (1812–1896) in the late nineteenth century. The baron, a well-known Parisian
bibliophile and collector, incorporated the paneling,
stripped of its original paint, into the large library
that he installed on the first floor of his Paris residence, the Hôtel Lauzun, at 17 quai d'Anjou, on the
Île Saint-Louis. The paneling, which dates from the
early Louis XVI period, about 1770, was not in keeping with the seventeenth-century decor of the Hôtel
Lauzun and was dismantled and sold by the baron's
grandson in 1906–7. The three doorways and the
pilasters were part of the woodwork installed in the
library at the Hôtel Lauzun. The three grisaille over-
door paintings in the style of Piat-Joseph Sauvage
(1744–1818), the white marble chimneypiece, and its
framed overmantel mirror are contemporary with but
not original to the room. The plaster cornice and ceiling rosette are modern.

The Client

Suit (*Habit à la française*). American, ca. 1780. Pale
blue silk with rose and white linear serpentine brocade and metal *paillette* embroidery. Rogers Fund,
1942 (42.105.1a–c)

Jewel Coffer on Stand (*Coffre à bijoux*). French, 1770.
Attributed to Martin Carlin (ca. 1730–1785). Oak
veneered with tulipwood, amaranth, sycamore, and
holly, Sèvres porcelain plaques, gilt bronze. Most
plaques with date letter for 1770 and with mark of
the painter Jean-Jacques Pierre the Younger (active
1763–92). Gift of the Samuel H. Kress Foundation,
1958 (58.75.41)

The Client's Wife

Dress (*Robe à la polonaise*). French, ca. 1780. Hand-
painted white Chinese silk. Purchase, Mr. and Mrs.
Alan S. Davis Gift, 1976 (1976.146a, b)

Small Desk (*Bonheur du jour*). French, ca. 1775.
Martin Carlin (ca. 1730–1785). Oak veneered with
tulipwood, purplewood, and sycamore, Sèvres porcelain plaques, gilt bronze. Most plaques with date
letter for 1774 and with mark of the painter Jean-
Jacques Pierre the Younger (active 1763–92). Gift of
the Samuel H. Kress Foundation, 1958 (58.75.49)

The Merchant

Suit (*Habit à la française*). French, 1775–80. Rose silk
with multicolored silk, gold *filé*, and *paillette* embroidery. Gift of International Business Machines
Corporation, 1960 (C.I.60.22.1a–c)

Paneling (*Boiserie*). Carved oak with modern paint.
French, ca. 1770. Purchase, Mr. and Mrs. Charles
Wrightsman Gift, 1976 (1976.91.1, 2)

Room from a Hôtel on the Cours d'Albret, Bordeaux (ca. 1785)

The delicate low-relief carving of the pine wall panels
is attributed to the sculptor and woodcarver
Barthélemy Cabirol (ca. 1732–1786) and his workshop. Born in Bordeaux, Cabirol is known to have
undertaken the decoration of many residences in the
city. He may have been responsible for the interiors
of the Hôtel de Saint-Marc, on the cours d'Albret,
constructed between 1782 and 1784. The Museum's
room may have come from this building, which is
now the Centre Hospitalier Régional de Bordeaux.
The Carrara marble chimneypiece and the *parquet de
Versailles* floor are contemporary with but not original
to the room.

The Abbé

Suit. French, 1775–80. Black silk taffeta. Courtesy of
Lillian Williams

Side chair (*Voyeuse*). French, ca. 1780–90. Attributed
to Sulpice Brizard (ca. 1735–1798). Carved, painted,
and gilded beech, modern rose *moiré* wool tabby.
Gift of Mrs. Ralph K. Robertson, 1969 (69.102.3)

Female Card Player 1

Dress (*Robe à la française*). French, 1775–80. Salmon,
burgundy, blue and white striped silk *cannelé* with
self-fabric *bouillonné* and ruched trim. Purchase,
Irene Lewisohn Bequest, 1960 (C.I.60.39.1a, b)

Armchair (*Fauteuil en cabriolet*). French, ca. 1785.
Carved beech, originally gilded, modern green
brocaded silk. Rogers Fund, 1926 (26.227.1)

Male Card Player 1

Suit (*Habit à la française*). French, 1778–85. Ivory, pale
pink, and brown silk *cannelé* with multicolored floral
silk embroidery. Fletcher Fund, 1961 (C.I.61.14.2a–c)

Side Chair (*Chaise en cabriolet*). French, 1775–80.
Jean-Baptiste II Lelarge (1743–1802). Carved and
gilded beech, modern green silk *cannelé*. Rogers
Fund, 1923 (23.147.2)

THE LATE SUPPER: THE MEMENTO

THE SHOP: THE OBSTRUCTION

Female Card Player 2

Dress (*Robe à la française*). French, 1775–80. Moss green, brown, ivory, and pale pinstriped silk taffeta with self-fabric *bouillonné* and ruched trim. Purchase, Irene Lewisohn Bequest, 1960 (C.I.60.39.2a, b)

Armchair (*Fauteuil en cabriolet*). French, ca. 1785. Pierre Brizard (ca. 1737–1804). Carved, painted, and gilded beech, modern rose silk velvet. Rogers Fund, 1926 (26.227.2)

Male Card Player 2

Suit (*Habit à la française*). French, late eighteenth century. Slate blue and brown ribbed silk, ivory silk satin with multicolored chenille and floral silk embroidery. Gift of Mrs. Frank A. Zunino Jr., 1966 (C.I.66.1.2a–c)

Side Chair (*Chaise en cabriolet*). French, 1775–80. Jean-Baptiste III Lelarge (1743–1802). Carved and gilded beech, modern green silk *cannelé*. Rogers Fund, 1923 (23.147.3)

Folding Card Table (*Table à jouer*). French, ca. 1755–65. Attributed to Bernard II van Risenburgh (1696–1766). Oak veneered with tulipwood, purple-wood, kingwood, *bois satiné*, and walnut, gilt bronze mounts, modern green felt. Gift of Mr. and Mrs. Charles Wrightsman, 1983 (1983.185.3)

Paneling (*Boiserie*). French, ca. 1785. Attributed to Barthélemy Cabirol (ca. 1732–1786). Carved and painted pine. Gift of Mrs. Herbert N. Straus, 1943 (43.158.1)

Room from the Hôtel de Crillon, Paris (ca. 1777–80)

This oak room came from the Hôtel de Crillon, at 10 place de la Concorde, Paris. It was built between 1755 and 1775 after designs by the architect Ange-Jacques Gabriel (1698–1782). Louis-Marie-Augustin, duc d'Aumont (1709–1782), a well-known collector of the period, lived in the Hôtel de Crillon from 1777 to 1782, and the decoration of the Museum's room was probably carried out for him between 1777 and 1780. The architect Pierre-Adrien Pâris (1747–1819) designed the decoration of the wall panels, which were executed by an unknown artist.

The Voluptuary

Dress (*Robe à la française*). French, late eighteenth century. Hand-painted green-and-white woven striped silk taffeta. Purchase, Irene Lewisohn Bequest, 1954 (C.I.54.70 a, b)

Stays. French, late eighteenth century. Cream silk with pink silk trim. Courtesy of Lillian Williams

Garter Ribbon. French, last quarter of the eighteenth century. Green silk taffeta. Courtesy of Lillian Williams

Daybed (*Sultane*) and Armchair (*Bergère*). French, 1788. Jean-Baptiste-Claude Sené (1748–1803). Carved, painted, and gilded walnut, modern green silk satin damask. Gift of Ann Payne Blumenthal, 1941 (41.205.1, .2)

The Libertine

Suit (*Habit à la française*). Italian, 1770–80. Chartreuse silk satin with rose and beige silk floral embroidery. Purchase, Rogers Fund, 1926 (26.56.63a–c)

Paneling (*Boiserie*). French, 1777–80. After designs by Pierre-Adrien Pâris (1747–1819). Painted and gilded oak. Gift of Susan Dwight Bliss, 1944 (44.128)

Shop Front From Île Saint-Louis, Paris (ca. 1775–77)

The shop front from 3 quai de Bourbon, on the north bank of the Île Saint-Louis, Paris, near the Pont Marie, was built by Étienne Séjournant between 1775 and 1777. It was superimposed on the masonry of an existing mid-seventeenth-century building and was removed from its original site during World War I.

The Girl in Flight

Dress (*Robe à l'anglaise*). European, mid-to-late eighteenth century. Ivory silk taffeta. Purchase, Irene Lewisohn Bequest, 1972 (1972.139.2)

The Reckless Suitor

Suit (*Habit à la française*). European, last quarter of the eighteenth century. Black wool with multicolored silk floral embroidery. Gift of Mr. Lee Simonson, 1939 (C.I.39.13.29)

Illustrations

[Page 6] François Boucher (French, 1703–1770). *Madame de Pompadour*, 1756. Oil on canvas. Die Alte Pinakothek, Munich. Photograph courtesy of The Bridgeman Art Library

[Page 8] Attributed to Elisabeth Vigée-LeBrun (French, 1755–1842). *Marie-Antoinette*, ca. 1783. Oil on canvas. Timken Collection, National Gallery of Art. Image © Board of Trustees, National Gallery of Art, Washington, DC

[Page 10] Jean-Honoré Fragonard (French, 1732–1806). Detail of *The Stolen Kiss*, ca. 1786–88. Oil on canvas. The State Hermitage Museum, St. Petersburg. Photograph courtesy of Erich Lessing / Art Resource, NY

[Page 13] Jean-Honoré Fragonard (French, 1732–1806). Detail of *The Bolt*, ca. 1777. Oil on canvas. Louvre, Paris. Photograph courtesy of Erich Lessing / Art Resource, NY

[Page 14] Jean-François de Troy (French, 1679–1752). Detail of *The Reading from Molière*, ca. 1728. Oil on canvas. Private Collection. Photograph courtesy of The Bridgeman Art Library

[Page 18] Jean-Michel Moreau le Jeune (French, 1741–1814). *Le Souper fin*, engraved by Isadore-Stanislas Helman (French, 1743–1806), from *Le Monument du costume*, 1781. Etching and engraving. The Metropolitan Museum of Art, Bequest of George Blumenthal, 1941 (41.140.7)

[Page 21] Nicolas Lavreince II (French, 1732–1807). *Qu'en dit l'abbé?*, engraved by Nicolas Delaunay (French, 1739–1792), 1788. Etching and engraving. The Metropolitan Museum of Art, Harris Brisbane Dick Fund, 1954 (54.533.17)

[Page 24] Adélaïde Labille-Guiard (French, 1749–1803). *Self-Portrait with Two Pupils, Mademoiselle Marie Gabrielle Capet* (1761–1818) *and Mademoiselle Carreaux de Rosemond* (d. 1788), 1785. Oil on canvas. The Metropolitan Museum of Art, Gift of Julia A. Berwind, 1953 (53.225.5)

[Page 27] Louis-Michel van Loo (French, 1707–1771). *Denis Diderot*, 1767. Oil on canvas. Louvre, Paris. Photograph courtesy of Erich Lessing / Art Resource, NY

[Page 34] Louis-Roland Trinquesse (French, ca. 1746–1800). Detail of *Interior Scene with Two Women and a Gentleman*, 1776. Oil on canvas. Maurice Segoura Collection

[Page 37] François Boucher (French, 1703–1770). *Jeanne-Antoinette Poisson, Marquise de Pompadour*, 1758. Oil on canvas. Courtesy of the Fogg Art Museum, Harvard University Art Museums, Bequest of Charles E. Dunlap, 1966.47. Photograph by Katya Kallsen. Image © 2004 President and Fellows of Harvard College

[Page 44] Jean-Michel Moreau le Jeune (French, 1741–1814). *L'Accord parfait*, engraved by Isadore-Stanislas Helman (French, 1743–1806), from *Le Monument du costume*, 1777. Etching and engraving. The Metropolitan Museum of Art, Harris Brisbane Dick Fund, 1933 (33.6.21)

[Page 47] Rose Adélaïde Ducreux (French, 1761–1802). *Self-Portrait with a Harp*, ca. 1790. Oil on canvas. The Metropolitan Museum of Art, Bequest of Susan Dwight Bliss, 1966 (67.55.1)

[Page 58] Augustin de Saint-Aubin (French, 1736–1807). Detail of *Le Bal paré*, etched by Antoine-Jean Duclos (French, 1742–1795), 1774. Etching. The Metropolitan Museum of Art, Harris Brisbane Dick Fund, 1933 (33.56.33)

[Page 61] François Boucher (French, 1703–1770). *Madame de Pompadour*, 1759. Oil on canvas. The Wallace Collection, London. Photograph courtesy of The Bridgeman Art Library

[Page 76] Jean-Michel Moreau le Jeune (French, 1741–1814). *Les Adieux*, engraved by Robert Delaunay (French, 1749–1814), from *Le Monument du costume*, 1777. Etching and engraving. The Metropolitan Museum of Art, Harris Brisbane Dick Fund, 1934 (34.22.1)

[Page 79] Charles Nicolas Cochin II (French, 1715–1790). Detail of *Masked Ball (Bal des Ifs) in honour of the marriage of Louis, the Dauphin of France, to María Theresa of Spain at Versailles (Galerie des Glaces)* on February 1745. Pen and brown ink with watercolor and white heightening. Louvre, Paris. Photograph by M. Bellot courtesy of Réunion des Musées Nationaux / Art Resource, NY

[Page 82] Hyacinthe Rigaud (French, 1659–1743). *Louis XV* (1710–1774) *as a Child*, ca. 1715–24. Oil on canvas. The Metropolitan Museum of Art, Purchase, Mary Wetmore Shively Bequest, in memory of her husband, Henry L. Shively, M.D., 1960 (60.6)

[Page 85] François-Hubert Drouais (French, 1727–1775). *Marie-Jeanne Bécu, Madame du Barry*, ca. 1770. Oil on canvas. Timken Collection, National Gallery of Art. Image © Board of Trustees, National Gallery of Art, Washington, DC

[Page 88] Jean-Antoine Watteau (French, 1684–1721). Detail of *Gersaint's Shop Sign*, 1720. Oil on canvas. Schloss Charlottenburg, Berlin. Stiftung Preußische Schlösser und Gärten Berlin-Brandenburg/Fotograf

[Page 91] Michel Garnier (French, 1753–1819). *The Poorly Defended Rose*, 1789. Oil on canvas. The Minneapolis Institute of Arts, Gift of Mr. and Mrs. Jack Linsky

[Page 98] Pierre Louis Dumesnil le Jeune (French, 1698–1781). Detail of *Interior with Card Players*, ca. 1750–60. Oil on canvas. The Metropolitan Museum of Art, Bequest of Harry G. Sperling, 1971 (1976.100.8)

[Page 101] Jean-Michel Moreau le Jeune (French, 1741–1814). *La Partie de whist*, engraved by Jean Dambrun (French, 1741–after 1808), from *Le Monument du costume*, 1788. Etching and engraving. The Metropolitan Museum of Art, Harris Brisbane Dick Fund, 1933 (33.6.12)

[Page 108] Jean-François de Troy (French, 1679–1752). *The Garter*, 1724. Oil on canvas. Private Collection, New York

[Page 111] Jean-François de Troy (French, 1679–1752). *The Declaration of Love*, 1724. Oil on canvas. Private Collection, New York

[Page 124] Jean-Honoré Fragonard (French, 1732–1806). *Young Woman Reading*, ca. 1780. Oil on canvas. The Metropolitan Museum of Art, Gift of René Fribourg, 1953 (53.161)

[Page 126] Jean-Michel Moreau le Jeune (French, 1741–1814). *N'Ayez pas peur ma bonne amie*, engraved by Isadore-Stanislas Helman (French, 1743–1806), from *Le Monument du costume*, 1776. Etching and engraving. The Metropolitan Museum of Art, Harris Brisbane Dick Fund, 1933 (33.6.19)

Select Bibliography

Bailey, Colin B., Philip Conisbee, and Thomas W. Gaehtgens. *The Age of Watteau, Chardin, and Fragonard: Masterpieces of French Genre Painting.* Exh. cat. New Haven: Yale University Press in association with the National Gallery of Canada, Ottawa, 2003.

Bastide, Jean-François de. *The Little House: An Architectural Seduction.* Translated by Rodolphe el-Khoury. New York: Princeton Architectural Press, 1996.

Batchelor, Jennie. *Dress, Distress, and Desire: Clothing and the Female Body in Eighteenth-Century Literature.* New York: Palgrave Macmillan, 2005.

Bernier, Olivier. *The Eighteenth-Century Woman.* Exh. cat. New York: The Metropolitan Museum of Art, 1981.

Cohen, Sarah R. *Art, Dance, and the Body in French Culture of the Ancien Régime.* Cambridge: Cambridge University Press, 2000.

Craveri, Benedetta. *The Age of Conversation.* Translated by Teresa Waugh. New York: New York Review Books, 2005.

Delpierre, Madeleine. *Dress in France in the Eighteenth Century.* New Haven: Yale University Press, 1997.

Edwards, Samuel. *The Divine Mistress.* London: Cassell, 1970.

Fairweather, Maria. *Madame De Staël.* New York: Carroll & Graf Publishers, 2005.

Feher, Michel. *The Libertine Reader: Eroticism and Enlightenment in Eighteenth-Century France.* New York: Zone Books, 1997.

Fukai, Akiko, ed. *FASHION: The Collection of the Kyoto Costume Institute. A History from the 18th to the 20th Century.* Cologne and London: Taschen, 2002.

Hart, Avril, and Susan North. *Historical Fashion in Detail: The 17th and 18th Centuries.* London: V&A Publications, 1998.

Haslip, Joan. *Madame Du Barry: The Wages of Beauty.* London: I. B. Tauris, 2005.

Hellman, Mimi. "Furniture, Sociability, and the Work of Leisure in Eighteenth-Century France." *Eighteenth-Century Studies* 32, no. 4 (1999), pp. 415–45.

Jones, Colin. *Madame de Pompadour: Images of a Mistress.* Exh. cat. London: National Gallery Company, 2002.

Jones, Jennifer M. *Sexing La Mode: Gender, Fashion, and Commercial Culture in Old Regime France.* Oxford and New York: Berg, 2004.

Kavanagh, Thomas M. *Enlightenment and the Shadows of Chance: The Novel and the Culture of Gambling in Eighteenth-Century France.* Baltimore: Johns Hopkins University Press, 1993.

Koda, Harold. *Extreme Beauty: The Body Transformed.* Exh. cat. New York: The Metropolitan Museum of Art, 2001.

Le Bourhis, Katell, ed. *The Age of Napoleon: Costume from Revolution to Empire 1789–1815.* Exh. cat. New York: The Metropolitan Museum of Art, 1989.

Leppert, Richard D. *Music and Image: Domesticity, Ideology and Socio-Cultural Formation in Eighteenth-Century England.* Cambridge: Cambridge University Press, 1988.

Maeder, Edward. *An Elegant Art: Fashion and Fantasy in the Eighteenth Century. Los Angeles County Museum of Art Collection of Costumes and Textiles.* Exh. cat. Los Angeles: Los Angeles County Museum of Art, 1983.

Martin, Richard. *The Ceaseless Century: 300 Years of Eighteenth-Century Costume.* Exh. cat. New York: The Metropolitan Museum of Art, 1998.

May, Gita. *Elisabeth Vigée Le Brun: The Odyssey of an Artist in an Age of Revolution.* New Haven: Yale University Press, 2005.

Metropolitan Museum of Art. *Period Rooms in The Metropolitan Museum of Art.* Contributions by Amelia Peck et al. New York: The Metropolitan Museum of Art, 1996.

Queneau, Jacqueline, and Jean-Yves Patte. *La France au temps des libertins.* Paris: Éditions du Chêne, 2001.

Rand, Richard, with Juliette M. Bianco. *Intimate Encounters: Love and Domesticity in Eighteenth-Century France.* Exh. cat. Hanover: Hood Museum of Art, Dartmouth College, 1997.

Ribeiro, Aileen. *The Art of Dress: Fashion in England and France, 1750–1820.* New Haven: Yale University Press, 1995.

Ribeiro, Aileen. *Dress in Eighteenth-Century Europe, 1715–1789.* Rev. ed. New Haven: Yale University Press, 2002.

Sargentson, Carolyn. *Merchants and Luxury Markets: The Marchands Merciers of Eighteenth-Century Paris.* London: Victoria and Albert Museum, 1996.

Scott, Katie. *The Rococo Interior: Decoration and Social Spaces in Early Eighteenth-Century Paris.* New Haven: Yale University Press, 1995.

Whitehead, John. *The French Interior in the Eighteenth Century.* London: Laurence King, 1992.

We are grateful to the many people who provided generous support for the exhibition "Dangerous Liaisons" and this handsome publication. In particular we are fortunate to have had the advice and encouragement of Philippe de Montebello, director of The Metropolitan Museum of Art; Emily K. Rafferty, president of The Metropolitan Museum of Art; Nina McN. Diefenbach, vice president for Development and Membership; Ian Wardropper, Iris and B. Gerald Cantor Chairman, European Sculpture and Decorative Arts; Daniëlle O. Kisluk-Grosheide, curator, European Sculpture and Decorative Arts; Mrs. Charles Wrightsman; Anna Wintour, editor in chief of American *Vogue*; and Asprey of London, who generously donated funds to the exhibition and this catalogue. We also thank Condé Nast for providing additional support for both projects.

Patrick Kinmonth, creative consultant, was responsible for staging the room vignettes that made the exhibition such a success and this book so striking. He was assisted by Josephine Pickett Baker, Chris Redman, Alison Walker, and Campbell Young.

Our colleagues in The Costume Institute have been invaluable in every aspect. We extend our deepest gratitude to Torrey Thomas Acri, Gail Anderson, Nick Barberio, Shannon Bell Price, Kitty Benton, Barbara Brickman, Elizabeth Bryan, Jane Butler, Beth Dincuff Charleston, Dina Cohen, Elyssa Da Cruz, Michael Downer, Andrew Drabkin, Jamilla Dunn, Eileen Ekstract, Lisa Faibish, Joyce Fung, Susan Furlaud, Jessica Glasscock, Charles Hansen, Stéphane Houy-Towner, Elizabeth Hyman, Betsy Kallop, Elizabeth Arpel Kehler, Susan Klein, Jessa Krick, Elizabeth Larson, Susan Lauren, Nina Libin, Joan Lufrano, Rena Lustberg, Melissa Marra, Bethany Matia, Veronica McNiff, Butzi Moffitt, Elizabeth Monks, Marci Morimoto, Doris Nathanson, Ellen Needham, Wendy Nolan, Julia Orron, Tatyana Pakhladzhyan, Christine Paulocik, Pat Peterson, Christine Petschek, Janina Poskrobko, Martin Price, Jan Reeder, Jessica Regan, Laurie Riley, Christine Ritschel, Eleanor Schloss, Lita Semerad, Rebecca Shea, Nancy Silbert, Katherine Smith, Judith Sommer, Heather Vaughn, Stacey N. Wacknov, Muriel Washer, Bernice Weinblatt, DJ White, the Visiting Committee, and the Friends of The Costume Institute.

Members of the Department of European Sculpture and Decorative Arts contributed generously of their time and knowledge, and we are indebted to Shirley Allison, Miro T. Bullo, Thomas P. Campbell, Vanessa Davidson, James David Draper, Patricia Flores, Cybèle Gontar, Roger Haapala, Marva Harvey, Johanna Hecht, Robert Kaufmann, Lorraine Karafel, Wolfram Koeppe, William Kopp, Jessie McNab, Jeffrey Munger, Marina Nudel, Stephanie Post, Eric Peluso, Erin E. Pick, William Rieder, Clare Vincent, Melinda Watt, and Rose Whitehill.

We are also grateful to members of the Textile Conservation staff, including Cristina Carr, Kathrin Colburn, Emilia Cortes, Min-Sun Hwang, Kristine Kamiya, Maya Naunton, Elena Phipps, Midori Sato, and Florica Zaharia.

Photographers Joseph Coscia Jr. and Oi-Cheong Lee, of the Photograph Studio of The Metropolitan Museum of Art, are to be commended for their successful translation of the vignettes into photographs that enhance the pages of this volume.

The Editorial Department of The Metropolitan Museum of Art, under the guidance of John P. O'Neill, editor in chief, provided the expertise to make this book a reality. Special thanks go to

Margaret R. Chace, Joan Holt, Gwen Roginsky, and Paula Torres. The design was carried out in extraordinary fashion by Takaaki Matsumoto, assisted by Amy Wilkins, Keith Price, and Hisami Aoki.

We would also like to thank colleagues from various departments at The Metropolitan Museum of Art for their assistance, including Rosayn D. Anderson, Katharine Baetjer, Kay Bearman, Pamela T. Barr, Renee Barrick, Mechthild Baumeister, Christine S. Begley, Eti Bonn-Muller, Barbara Bridgers, Nancy C. Britton, Eugenia Burnett Tinsley, Cindy Caplan, Andrew Caputo, Jennie Choi, Aileen K. Chuk, Michael Cocherell, Clint Coller, Sharon H. Cott, Teresa Christiansen, Deanna Cross, Willa M. Cox, Jeffrey Daly, Jennifer Dodge, Marian Eines, Priscilla F. Farah, Catherine Fukashimi, Helen Garfield, Patricia Gilkison, Claire Gylphé, Herbert Heyde, Harold Holzer, Catherine Jenkins, Michael Jenkins, Marilyn Jensen, Andrea Kann, Phyllis Keilson, Anna-Marie Kellen, Beth Kovalsky, Bernice Kwok-Gabel, Alexandra Klein, Michael Langley, Kerstin Larsen, Laurence Libin, Richard Lichte, Thomas Ling, Amanda Maloney, Kristin M. MacDonald, Nina S. Maruca, Missy McHugh, Constance McPhee, Susan Melick Bresnan, Taylor Miller, J. Kenneth Moore, Mark Morosse, Herbert M. Moskowitz, Rebecca L. Murray, Nadine Orenstein, Sally Pearson, Joseph Peknik III, Blanche Perris Kahn, Diana Pitt, Doralynn Pines, Stewart S. Pollens, Lucinda K. Ross, Nancy Rutledge, Christine Scornavacca, Kenneth Soehner, Linda Sylling, Elyse Topalian, Valerie Troyansky, Philip T. Venturino, Barbara Weiss, Karin L. Willis, Deborah Winshel, Heather Woodworth, Steve Zane, and Elizabeth Zanis.

We are extremely grateful to the lenders to the exhibition not only for their loans to the show but also for allowing us to reproduce their costumes on the following pages. Our thanks go to: Colonial Williamsburg Foundation, the Costume Design Center (Brenda Rosseau), Colonial Williamsburg Foundation, the Shoemaking Program (James Gaynor, Al Saguto), John England (Textiles) Ltd, the Kyoto Costume Institute (Akiko Fukai, Jun Kanai, Tamami Suoh, Rie Nii), Pennsylvania State University Library (Sandra Stelts), Frederick P. Victoria & Sons, Inc. (Anthony G. Victoria), and Lillian Williams.

Special thanks are due to Oriole Cullen, David Vincent, and Charlotte Crosby Nicklas.